BAD
TO THE
BONE

# Books by Miles McPherson

21 Jump-Start Devotional

Bad to the Bone

The Power of Believing in Your Child

# BAD
## TO THE
# BONE

**FIFTEEN YOUNG BIBLE HEROES WHO
LIVED RADICAL LIVES FOR GOD**

# MILES MCPHERSON

**BETHANY HOUSE PUBLISHERS**
MINNEAPOLIS, MINNESOTA 55438

Published by Bethany House Publishers
A Ministry of Bethany Fellowship International
11400 Hampshire Avenue South
Minneapolis, Minnesota 55438
www.bethanyhouse.com

Printed in the United States of America by
Bethany Press International, Minneapolis, Minnesota 55438

**Library of Congress Cataloging-in-Publication Data**

McPherson, Miles.
    Bad to the bone : fifteen cool Bible heroes who lived radical lives for God / by Miles McPherson.
        p.    cm.
    Summary: Tells the stories of young biblical heroes who were not afraid to reject evil and to turn their lives over to God and suggests ways to respond to these accounts.
    ISBN 0-7642-2280-5 (pbk.)
    1. Teenagers—Prayer-books and devotions—English.  2. Heroes in the Bible—Prayer-books and devotions—English.  3. Devotional calendars.  [1. Prayer books and devotions.  2. Heroes in the Bible.  3. Devotional calendars.]  I. Title.
BV4850.M33    1999                                 99–6529
242'.63—dc21                                      CIP

This book is dedicated
to all the young people who

- have a sincere desire to be all Christ wants them to be
- are tired of being hypocrites and want to be on fire for God
- want to see miracles happen in their lives
- want to stand up against the pressure to follow the crowd
- want to develop and use their spiritual gifts to the level of God's expectation
- have a sincere desire to be used by God to build His kingdom
- love God and want to be bad to the bone.

MILES McPHERSON is a former NFL football player with the San Diego Chargers, nationally known youth evangelist, and president of Miles Ahead Ministries. His city-wide youth evangelistic events, the Miles Ahead Crusades, have seen over 15,000 teenagers make commitments to Jesus Christ. He teaches two weekly services at Horizon Christian Fellowship to over 2,800 bad-to-the-bone believers. Miles has a sincere desire himself to be bad to the bone. He and his family reside in San Diego, California.

# CONTENTS

# INTRODUCTION

What ran through your head when you saw the title of this book, *Bad to the Bone*? If you know George Thorogood's classic rock song of the same name, did you wonder, *Who would name a Christian book after a song about rebellious, wild living?*

Me.

And here's why. Because if you're going to fulfill God's calling for your life, being rebellious is a very necessary thing—as long as you're rebelling against the right things.

I wrote this devotional because I want you to be a Christian rebel. Fact is, God wants you to be a rebel. Want proof? Just check out the Bible, God's how-to manual for us. It's filled with young people who lived wild and crazy lives—for God. They threw caution to the wind and allowed God to use them in supernatural ways. They were bad to the bone.

- 🏃 Josiah was bad to the bone when, at sixteen, he began to seek God on his own in order to bring about a national revival. He announced to the whole country, "I'm reading my Bible, and so will you."
- 🏃 Esther was bad to the bone when, as a teenager, she confronted the king about the death sentence on her people. Esther knew she was good-looking, and used her beauty to save a race of people.
- 🏃 Joseph was bad to the bone when, at seventeen, he believed in God's dream that he would become one of the most powerful men in the world. Joseph proclaimed to his family, "One day I'm going to be DA MAN!"
- 🏃 Shadrach, Meshach, and Abed-Nego were bad to the bone when, as young people, they defied the king's orders to bow to his idol. In essence, they asked the angry king, "What part of 'we will not bow' don't you understand?"
- 🏃 David was bad to the bone when, as a teenager, he killed Goliath with

one rock—and talked trash all the while, telling Goliath that he was going to kill him, cut off his head, and kill the entire Philistine army. Think about it, David only had five rocks.

✗ Daniel was bad to the bone when, as a teenager, he denied the king's delicacies and instead ate vegetables and water. Daniel knew that the Twinkies would eventually kill him.

✗ Jesus was bad to the bone when, at the age of twelve, He hung out and challenged the temple rabbis to a debate on the Bible, God's Word. Fools. Jesus IS the Word, so they didn't stand a chance.

✗ Rebekah was bad to the bone when she left her family on a minute's notice to marry Isaac, the man who would father Israel himself. Her true love did not need to wait any longer.

These and other kids in the Bible could not be killed, discouraged, beat down, or defeated in any way. They were invincible, incredible, and indestructible. They were committed to God all the way down to the bone.

So what does all this mean for you and me?

God hasn't changed His tune from Bible times. He's still looking for people who are not afraid to go against the junk of this world; kids who are not afraid of being singled out for being godly, resisting the temptations of teenage life, and being sold out for Jesus.

*For the eyes of the Lord run to and fro throughout the whole earth, to show Himself strong on behalf of those whose heart is loyal to Him.*

*—2 Chronicles 16:9*

Are you loyal to the Lord, saying no to sinful ways? Does "No Fear" describe your life in Christ? If so, great. If not, what's holding you back?

In my ministry I meet and get to know all sorts of young people. Let me tell you, lots of kids are living flat-out for God. But many others are really struggling. They may not fess up, but they're hurting because of poor choices they've made. Do you know what these two groups have in common? Someone in their life is either being a positive influence or a negative one. And you know *which* influence usually leads to *what*.

For the next thirteen weeks I want you to be influenced by some young people who lived radical lives for God. I want to challenge you, inspire you, encourage you. I want you to live an out-of-this-world life of faith like they did. Not for my sake. For your sake and God's. And here's how we're going to do it.

Each week, Monday through Friday, we'll focus on someone from the Bible whom I call a "Be Like" person. These are young heroes whom we should all strive to be like: people such as Joseph, who was a godly dreamer; Mary, who was holy; and Josiah, who was on fire for the Lord. In all, you'll get to better know fifteen "Be Like" teens during the thirteen weeks. (Week 11 features three bad-to-the-bone buddies: Shadrach, Meshach, and Abed-Nego.)

Memorizing Scripture is a major part of living for Christ, so each week I'll ask you to memorize a key verse. The more Scripture you know and place your trust in, the stronger your faith will become.

For each day I suggest a reading from the Bible. (Sometimes, to encourage you to dig deeper into a passage, the same verses will be used more than once.) After a brief devotional—sort of my take on the Scripture reading—it's your turn for action, or better yet, *interaction*. I'm going to put you on the spot, asking you to compare your attitude, actions—you name it—with those of that week's Bible hero. Then I follow up with a prayer to jump-start your conversation with God.

Now, this devotional is set up primarily to be used Monday through Friday. But rebels for God don't take weekends off. That's why I've included an important section each week called Weekend Warriors. Here, too, you'll learn about young people in the Bible. But there's a twist. Not all of them are positive role models; just like the kids around you today, some are living for God, others are not. Either way, you can still learn from their victories and their mistakes. There's another reason why I've included Weekend Warrior devotions, however. As you know, weekends, especially Friday and Saturday nights, are "dangerous" times for teenagers. You don't have to look hard for temptations at parties, on dates, or when you're just hanging out. Plain and simple, people are more likely to act wild on weekends, which is all the more reason to rebel against negative influences and instead be bad to the bone.

Over the next thirteen weeks and beyond, I hope and pray that this book will ignite a desire in you to be used in a supernatural way by God.

## THE FINE PRINT

Okay, before the truth police come knocking, I need to tell you that even though this book shines a spotlight on teenagers in the Bible, not everyone featured here is necessarily between the ages of thirteen and nineteen. Some are younger, such as Josiah, who at the age of eight became a king; and Jesus, who was only twelve when He was in the temple. For others, we don't know their exact ages, partly because Hebrew and Greek words for children are sometimes imprecise. In the case of young Timothy, it is unlikely that he was a teen when he ministered to Paul, but there are lessons he learned when he was a teenager that Paul built on. All in all, though, the stories in this book feature young people or the lessons they learned when they were young.

# WEEK 1

## Be Disciplined Like Daniel

Imagine your entire world being turned upside down. First, your parents are killed, then at the age of sixteen you are kidnapped and trained to serve a pagan king. In the process, you are ordered to eat food and drink wine that goes against your beliefs and spiritual convictions. What would you do? Go along with the crowd, or rebel against the king and his servants?

> *Daniel purposed in his heart that he would not defile himself with the portion of the king's delicacies, nor with the wine which he drank; therefore he requested of the chief of the eunuchs that he might not defile himself.*
>
> *—Daniel 1:8*

Daniel, one of the few people in the Bible who never received any bad press, knew that eating the king's delicacies would only lead to sin and compromise in his spiritual life. Daniel was way too committed to God for this to happen.

This week the Holy Spirit will challenge you to be bad-to-the-bone disciplined like Daniel. May God bless you as you study His Word this week.

# Memory Verse
# of the Week

Jesus said to him, "No one, having put his
hand to the plow, and looking back, is fit
for the kingdom of God."

LUKE 9:62

# MONDAY

## The Right Stuff

### Read Daniel 1:3–4

One summer, a group of NFL players and I conducted an outreach in south central Los Angeles. We visited several housing projects to share the Gospel. We went door to door, talked with gang members on the streets, and also addressed high school assemblies. One day, we conducted a football clinic in a nearby park for about fifty kids under the age of twelve. We had them line up and go through many of the drills done by NFL teams.

As the kids ran through the drills, I was amazed by the talent some of them had. One boy in particular could backpedal, spin, cut, and accelerate like some of the pros on our team. Not only did he have natural talent, he seemed to understand what he was doing. What really made him stand out, though, was his willingness to work hard and stay focused on what we were trying to teach. The kid was disciplined. And if I were picking a Pop Warner football team, he would be one of my first draftees.

Being disciplined may sound like fingernails on a chalkboard, but it always leads to good things. When Nebuchadnezzar invaded Israel,

*The king instructed Ashpenaz, the master of his eunuchs, to bring some of the children of Israel and some of the king's descendants and some of the nobles, young men in whom there was no blemish, but good-looking, gifted in all wisdom, possessing knowledge and quick to understand, who had ability to serve in the king's palace, and whom they might teach the language and literature of the Chaldeans.*

*—Daniel 1:3–4*

Nebuchadnezzar knew what he wanted; he knew what qualities a young man would need to serve him and his palace. And Daniel fit the bill. He had all the talent. He was good-looking, wise, and quick to learn. He ate right, was a good student, and was faithful to God. It was obvious to everyone that Daniel had his act together.

If Nebuchadnezzar invaded your town, would you be valuable enough to be kidnapped? Aren't sure? Do parts of your life need improving? Well, if you're not good enough for an earthly king, do you think you're good enough for a heavenly king? Yes, our heavenly Father is a forgiving God. He doesn't expect His children to be perfect. Still, God wants you and me to do our best for ourselves and Him. He wants to use noble men and women in His kingdom.

Make a commitment this week to be a noble young man or woman—one that is valuable in the hands of God. Make a commitment to ". . . stir up the gift of God which is in you through the laying on of my hands" (2 Timothy 1:6). Everything about you—your physical body, mental ability, emotions, and spiritual health—make up the temple of God, so it all deserves the best of care and a disciplined development. Make a commitment this week to be disciplined like Daniel.

## Interaction

What changes in attitude or actions do you think you need to adopt to make yourself a valuable tool in the hands of God?

## Prayer

*Dear Lord, thank you for your Word. I pray that you would help me strengthen my strengths and become a noble youth, one that you can depend on and one that you can use for much good in your kingdom. I pray that I could be bad-to-the-bone disciplined like Daniel. In Jesus' name I pray, Amen.*

## Memory Verse

Jesus said to him, "No one, having put his hand to the plow, and looking back, is fit for the kingdom of God."

Luke 9:62

# TUESDAY

## The Diet of the Disciplined

### Read Daniel 1

When I was a kid and wanting to grow up and play football, my father always told me to eat my vegetables. One problem, though. Vegetables weren't exactly a favorite of mine. The truth is, I hated them so much that I'd force myself to swallow them without even chewing. Down they went like an aspirin or a vitamin.

Broccoli was the worst. It was so chunky that I couldn't even swallow it whole. The only way to get rid of it was to sneak it to my sister, who would eat it for me. Go figure. Instead of vegetables, I thrived on ice cream. Consequently, I never did grow up to be big and strong.

When Daniel was threatened about eating the king's food, he decided instead to eat vegetables and water. Vegetables would bless his body, Daniel thought, and even make him wiser than all the other guys that Nebuchadnezzar was training to work in his palace. Daniel's diet supported his disciplined life. No, vegetables wouldn't necessarily make him smarter, but obedience to God would secure God's blessing.

What is your spiritual diet for success? Here's a simple one that is guaranteed to help you be disciplined like Daniel.

- First, make a commitment to be in constant communication and contact with God. Pray when you are walking to school, working out, or counseling a friend. Philippians 5:17 calls this praying without ceasing.
- Second, read and memorize God's Word. Psalm 119:9–11 says, "How can a young man cleanse his way? By taking heed according to Your word. With my whole heart I have sought You; Oh, let me not wander from Your commandments! Your word I have hidden in my heart, That I might not sin against You!"

- Third, stay in constant fellowship with Christians. Plant yourself at church. Hebrews 10:24–25 says, "And let us consider one another in order to stir up love and good works, not forsaking the assembling of ourselves together, as is the manner of some, but exhorting one another, and so much the more as you see the Day approaching."
- Fourth, commit yourself to being involved in ministry whether in a paid position or not. Ephesians 4:11–14 says, "And He Himself gave some to be apostles, some prophets, some evangelists, and some pastors and teachers, for the equipping of the saints for the work of ministry, for the edifying of the body of Christ, till we all come to the unity of the faith and of the knowledge of the Son of God, to a perfect man, to the measure of the stature of the fullness of Christ; that we should no longer be children, tossed to and fro and carried about with every wind of doctrine, by the trickery of men, in the cunning craftiness of deceitful plotting."

## Interaction

Describe how you can apply your own spiritual diet on a daily basis. Write out a schedule that will help you stay disciplined.

## Prayer

*Dear Lord, thank you for your Word. I pray that I can be disciplined and feed on your diet every day. I pray that I can depend and trust in your diet for spiritual health. I know if I do this every day, I will be bad-to-the-bone disciplined like Daniel. In Jesus' name I pray, Amen.*

## Memory Verse

Jesus said to him, "No one, having put his hand to the plow, and looking back, is fit for the kingdom of God."

Luke 9:62

# WEDNESDAY

## Satan's Delicacies

### Read Daniel 1

t seems like everyone—young and old—has at one time tried to lose weight by dieting. Sweets, treats, and, for some people, even meats, are suddenly off limits. Dieters are usually successful for a time, but without fail (usually around the holidays), their quest ends. Cakes, candies, and cookies prove to be too tempting.

Falling off a weight-loss diet is one thing. But falling off your spiritual diet results in much more dangerous consequences. Rather than adding inches to your waistline, it will add distance between you and God.

Satan will send many temptations your way in order to distract you from God's diet of prayer, Bible study, and fellowship with believers. You must be disciplined to stick to God's diet; wise enough to know what the Devil's delicacies look like.

When Daniel was kidnapped and offered Nebuchadnezzar's delicacies, he resisted. He knew what the king was up to. The king may have been offering tasty food, but only to lure Daniel away from being faithful to God. Daniel knew that if he ate the delicacies even once and liked them, he might get addicted to them and turn his back on the disciplined lifestyle God had given him.

Satan will offer you nice things, outrageous friends, and exciting parties not because he loves you, but because he wants to destroy you. He will tempt you to have sex, do drugs, or simply disobey God, any way he can. As Jesus says in John 10:10, "The thief does not come except to steal, and to kill, and to destroy. I have come that they may have life, and that they may have it more abundantly."

Satan is a murderer; he takes life away. So if you want to be disciplined like Daniel, you are going to have to purpose in your heart not to defile or poison yourself with Satan's delicacies.

## Interaction

Write down the top five delicacies, or temptations, that the devil is offering you, and then write down the trap he is setting for your life.

## Prayer

*Dear Lord, thank you for your Word. I pray that I would recognize the Devil's delicacies and that I would have the discipline to deny them and stick to your diet. I pray that even though the Devil is smart, through your wisdom I will be smarter. I am confident that you are able to keep me pure and bad-to-the-bone disciplined like Daniel. In Jesus' name I pray, Amen.*

## Memory Verse

Jesus said to him, "No one, having put his hand to the plow, and looking back, is fit for the kingdom of God."

Luke 9:62

# THURSDAY

## Hard Work

### Read Daniel 1

One of the dangers of being a determined, disciplined person is becoming a workaholic. You know the type—people so obsessed with work and being "successful" that they neglect other important things in their lives.

In the case of Daniel, he was chosen by King Nebuchadnezzar, along with many other young men, to be trained to work in the palace. The king wanted young men who exhibited intelligence and great understanding of the kingdom's culture and business. But Daniel knew that without the Lord's blessing, the work would be worthless. As Psalm 27:1 says, "Unless the Lord builds the house, they labor in vain who build it; unless the Lord guards the city, the watchman stays awake in vain."

Daniel stayed focused on God's work rather than the king's, so when Daniel decided to eat just vegetables, God blessed him with ten times more understanding than the others. Nebuchadnezzar's training and hard work were no match for Daniel's hard work that had God's blessing attached to it. Hard work is good, but hard work blessed by God is even better.

To get ahead in life, you'll need to work hard, but it must be done according to God's plan. It is important to be in constant contact with God to hear His instruction for your life and then work hard according to that instruction. If you read Daniel 1:17–20, you'll see the result of working with God's blessing. Do things God's way, be disciplined like Daniel, and you will receive God's wisdom and understanding.

### Interaction

In what way can you study your schoolwork and Bible differently in order to be more in line with God's way and receive His blessing?

## Prayer

*Dear Lord, thank you for your Word. I pray that I would be wise about how I work and study. I pray that I will not work just to get ahead. Please lead me by the hand, tell me when to turn right and turn left, that I may do your will effectively and efficiently. I know that if I do this, I will be bad-to-the-bone disciplined like Daniel. In Jesus' name I pray, Amen.*

## Memory Verse

Jesus said to him, "No one, having put his hand to the plow, and looking back, is fit for the kingdom of God."

Luke 9:62

# FRIDAY
## Secret Weapon
### Read Daniel 1

When I was shopping for my wife's diamond ring, I was blessed to meet a diamond cutter who showed me his craft. Cutting a rough diamond is an amazing process. Before a diamond is cut, it looks like rock candy—very cloudy and dirty, with rounded edges. But the diamond cutter is gifted. He can look through the cloudy rock and see which cuts are necessary to create a valuable stone.

After planning where the finished diamond's top, sides, and bottom will be, the diamond cutter puts the rough stone in a vice and begins to chip away unwanted pieces. Using precise tools, he slices, chisels, and shines something ugly into something truly beautiful—a diamond with special and unique qualities. It's the same way in the Lord's kingdom. God wants our special talents to shine. He has a plan for our lives.

*As for these four young men, God gave them knowledge and skill in all literature and wisdom; and Daniel had understanding in all visions and dreams.*

*—Daniel 1:17*

Daniel was given the unique ability to interpret dreams. And because he was disciplined and stuck to God's diet, he became a very skilled weapon in the hand of God. The question is, are there any rough spots in your life that need to be chiseled away in order for you to do awesome things for God?

If God went to war, how would He use you? What is your specialty? I ask because we *are* at war, a spiritual war. Spiritual forces of darkness oppose our efforts to please and serve God.

*For we do not wrestle against flesh and blood, but against principalities, against powers, against the rulers of the darkness of this age, against spiritual hosts of wickedness in the heavenly places.*

*—Ephesians 6:10*

If sin and other things in your life are hiding your God-given talents, you are probably doing Him little good in the battle. Challenge yourself to be disciplined like Daniel, allowing God to develop in you His special talents so that you might be pleasing to Him.

## Interaction

God has given you unique talents that are possible only through Him. Begin praying that He will reveal these gifts and provide opportunities to use them for His glory.

## Prayer

*Dear Lord, thank you for your Word. Please give me the eyes to see what role I play in your army. What talents have you given specifically to me? How should I be serving you? Show me in what area of my life I need to be bad-to-the-bone disciplined like Daniel so that my talents will shine. In Jesus' name I pray, Amen.*

## Memory Verse

Jesus said to him, "No one, having put his hand to the plow, and looking back, is fit for the kingdom of God."

Luke 9:62

# WEEKEND WARRIOR

## Ishmael

### Read Genesis 21: 1–21

**M**y brother was a professional boxer for over ten years. In that time, I developed a great respect for fighters, especially their never-give-up attitude. I'll never forget one amateur fight in which one of the boxers seemed to be getting beat to a pulp. In the first two rounds he was knocked down four times. When the third and final round started, it looked like it was going to be much of the same. Beat up, knocked down. Beat up, knocked down. At one point, the boxer's corner men yelled to see if he wanted to stop. He waved them off, though, got up, and promptly knocked his opponent out cold.

Like that boxer, things looked pretty grim for Ishmael in today's Bible reading. After being told to leave Abraham's home, he and his mother, Hagar, wandered in the desert until their food and water was gone. Knocked down and almost out, Hagar placed the boy under a bush.

*Then she went and sat down across from him at a distance of about a bowshot; for she said to herself, "Let me not see the death of the boy." So she sat opposite him, and lifted her voice and wept.*
*—Genesis 21:16*

Just then, God made a promise to Ishmael's mother: "Arise, lift up the lad and hold him with your hand, for I will make him a great nation" (Genesis 21:18). From then on, Ishmael's mom held on to the promises of God. She believed God would make Ishmael into a great nation. There was no reason to give up.

If there is one thing you can count on in hard times, it's God. Throughout the Bible, He promises us much.

*Let your conduct be without covetousness; be content with such things as you have. For He Himself has said, "I will never leave you nor forsake you."*

*—Hebrews 13:5*

*For I know the thoughts that I think toward you, says the Lord, thoughts of peace and not of evil, to give you a future and a hope.*

*—Jeremiah 29:11*

*Blessed be the God and Father of our Lord Jesus Christ, who has blessed us with every spiritual blessing in the heavenly places in Christ.*

*—Ephesians 1:3*

God is one hundred percent faithful to His promises. No matter the circumstance, He will never let you down—all the more reason to be disciplined in trusting God. So the next time things get rough and you feel like giving up, have faith in God's promises.

## Interaction

When you feel down and out, what do you do? Write down the promises that God has made to you. Then, write down a full-page description of what He has already done for you.

## Prayer

*Dear Lord, thank you for your Word. I pray that when I am down and out, I will remember your promises for us. I pray that you would reveal your special promises for my life. Give me the wisdom to know how to find them in your Word and that I will trust in them to become a bad-to-the-bone believer. In Jesus' name I pray, Amen.*

# WEEKEND WARRIOR

## Ishmael

### Read Genesis 21:1–21

I don't care who you are, where you live, what kind of family you have, or how much money is in your pocket or bank account, you will go through hard times in your life. I should know; I've been through them myself. Not surprisingly, it is during these times that Satan will mess with you by whispering lies in your ear. He will try to make you believe that everyone is against you. He will lie and say that even God is mad at you. When this happens, what are you going to do? Fall for the lies? Or cry out to God for help?

> *Let us therefore come boldly to the throne of grace, that we may obtain mercy and find grace to help in time of need.*
> *—Hebrews 4:16*

There you have it. Whenever we are in trouble, God wants us to go to Him. He wants to help. God knows where you are, how you're feeling, and what you're going through. Just look at what He did when Ishmael cried out in the desert.

> *And God heard the voice of the lad. Then the angel of God called to Hagar out of heaven, and said to her, "What ails you, Hagar? Fear not, for God has heard the voice of the lad where he is."*
> *—Genesis 21:17*

This weekend, while everyone else seems to be partying and having fun the Devil's way, you may feel tempted to join in. You might start hearing the voice of Satan. If this happens, keep in mind that you can always cry out to God.

> *No temptation has overtaken you except such as is common to*

*man; but God is faithful, who will not allow you to be tempted beyond what you are able, but with the temptation will also make the way of escape, that you may be able to bear it.*

*—1 Corinthians 10:13*

What a comforting promise. Not only will you be able to stand up under pressure, but you know that you're not alone; other people are facing the same temptations.

When Ishmael cried, God heard. When you cry out to Him, He will hear you also. The Bible encourages us to cast all of our cares on God because He cares for us. Do you believe that? Scripture also says that trials are good for our growth.

*My brethren, count it all joy when you fall into various trials, knowing that the testing of your faith produces patience. But let patience have its perfect work, that you may be perfect and complete, lacking nothing. If any of you lacks wisdom, let him ask of God, who gives to all liberally and without reproach, and it will be given to him.*

*—James 1:2–5*

When you are going through trials, call out to God, who gives wisdom without limit and hesitation. He wants you to grow through your problems.

## Interaction

Rather than complain in times of trouble, make a commitment to cry out to God. Write down what you will say so that when you face temptation or other challenges you'll be ready.

## Prayer

*Dear Lord, thank you for your Word. I pray that I will not be one to complain when, in my view, things go wrong. I pray that I will realize that you are trying to cause growth in my life. I pray that I will believe that you have given me the strength to stand under all pressure and that I am not the only one going through painful times. In Jesus' name I pray, Amen.*

# WEEK 2

## Be a Courageous Giant-Killer Like David

For forty days, one man—a nine-foot, nine-inch giant named Goliath—dared an entire army to send someone to fight him. For forty days not a single soldier accepted the challenge. Then a teenage shepherd boy named David flexed his muscles and did what no else would even attempt: He fought and killed the bully all by himself.

Some say it simply took a perfectly slung stone for David to become a giant-killer; however, his God-inspired courage deserves the real credit. David was no doubt scared of Goliath at first. Everyone else was. But David trusted God with all his heart, and in return, God transformed his fear into courage.

These days, there aren't too many nine-foot guys walking around picking fights. That doesn't mean we're safe, though. We need to beat down our own "giants" that take the form of sinful habits, negative attitudes from others, self-defeating thoughts, and so on. This week the Holy Spirit will challenge you to be a courageous, bad-to-the-bone giant-killer like David. May God bless you as you study His Word this week.

29

# Memory Verse of the Week

"Have I not commanded you? Be strong and of good courage; do not be afraid, nor be dismayed, for the Lord your God is with you wherever you go."

JOSHUA 1:9

# MONDAY

## The Boy/Man

### Read 1 Samuel 17

One day while some friends were staying at my house I noticed something very disturbing. All day the mother kept putting down her son with statements like "You'll never be able to do that." It was clear that she did not believe in her child's ability.

There will always be people in your life telling you what you can and cannot do. But no matter what others believe about your abilities, it does not excuse you from being obedient to God's call on your life.

When David prepared to fight Goliath, Saul told him he couldn't win. His reason: David was only a kid, and Goliath had been a man of war since his own childhood. Basically, Saul thought Goliath would beat David all over the field.

*Saul said to David, "You are not able to go against this Philistine to fight with him; for you are a youth, and he a man of war from his youth."*

*—1 Samuel 17:33*

Did you notice that Saul said Goliath was a man of war even as a youth? How can you be a man (or woman) and a youth at the same time? Well, the answer is simple: It depends on your level of courage in doing what you must do.

Immature, ungodly boys and girls pretty much do what they want to do and whine when they don't get their way. Mature, godly men and women do what they need to do for God, regardless of their personal desires. They have the courage to kill the giant obstacles of discouragement, doubt, and negative people in their lives to get God's job done.

If Satan could train a young Goliath to be a man of war when he was still a child, God can certainly train you now to be a godly man or woman. But you must be courageous enough to be obedient to Him in every little detail, not just when it's convenient for you. Courageous giant-killers obey God at all costs and at all times.

## Interaction

What ways would you say that you're acting like a child instead of a godly man or woman? Consider this question in regard to prayer, reading the Bible, obeying your parents, faithfulness on your job, and doing your homework. Write down how you need to be more obedient in order to become a courageous giant-killer for God.

## Prayer

*Dear Lord, thank you for your Word. I pray that my heart will always be pure in its desire to serve you. My prayer is that I would be responsible to do what you tell me to do. I know that obedience is more desirable than sacrifice. I know that you need fearless servants who are willing to obey you. I want to be that person. Only then can I serve you as a courageous, bad-to-the-bone giant-killer like David. In Jesus' name I pray, Amen.*

## Memory Verse

"Have I not commanded you? Be strong and of good courage; do not be afraid, nor be dismayed, for the Lord your God is with you wherever you go."

Joshua 1:9

# TUESDAY

## Used To Do's

### Read 1 Samuel 17

I t was the first day of school, and two guys, a sophomore and a freshman, were rushing to class. When they got behind a couple of girls, the freshman started to give them a hard time.

"What are you doing?" the sophomore angrily asked the freshman as he pulled him aside.

"Hey, what's up with you?" the freshman responded. "Relax. I used to do that all the time in junior high."

"Yeah, you *used to do* it, but grow up. We don't do that stuff here."

There comes a time in everyone's life when they must grow up and drop their old, immature ways. If you are doing things like gossiping, procrastinating, putting others down, or worrying about being popular with classmates rather than being with God, it's time to make a change. The same goes for adults. We all struggle with sinful habits that separate us from God. Sometimes, we even need to drop our worldly activities or responsibilities in order to do God's work.

When David heard the Israelites were in trouble, he left his flock with another shepherd and rushed to the battle line to help. Instead of receiving thanks, however, David was chewed out by his oldest brother, who asked, "Why did you come down here? And with whom have you left those few sheep in the wilderness?" (1 Samuel 17:28).

Even after volunteering to fight Goliath, David got no respect. King Saul told him, "You are not able to go against this Philistine to fight with him; for you are a youth, and he a man of war from his youth" (verse 33).

Yes, David was young and he *used to* keep his father's sheep, defending them from danger, but it was now time to defend his country in God's name.

*Your servant used to keep his father's sheep, and when a lion or a bear came and took a lamb out of the flock, I went out after it and struck it, and delivered the lamb from its mouth; and when it arose against me, I caught it by its beard, and struck and killed it. Your servant has killed both lion and bear; and this uncircumcised Philistine will be like one of them, seeing he has defied the armies of the living God.*

*—1 Samuel 17:34–36*

Right now God is calling you to slay the giants of your past, to drop any sinful habits, so that you can begin to follow Him into the future. As the apostle Paul said, "When I was a child, I spoke as a child, I understood as a child, I thought as a child; but when I became a man, I put away childish things" (1 Corinthians 13:11).

## Interaction

What nagging habit, sinful way, or distraction in your life do you need to get beyond in order to mature into a courageous giant-killer like David? As a sign of your commitment to change, write it down, tear it up, and throw it in the trash.

## Prayer

*Dear Lord, thank you for your Word. My prayer today is that I let go of all of my sinful habits and behaviors. I realize that if anyone is in Christ, the old is gone and the new has come. Help me to make my sinful habits "used to do's." I pray that I will recognize the immature areas of my life and grow up into the courageous, bad-to-the-bone giant-killer that David was. In Jesus' name I pray, Amen.*

## Memory Verse

"Have I not commanded you? Be strong and of good courage; do not be afraid, nor be dismayed, for the Lord your God is with you wherever you go."

Joshua 1:9

# WEDNESDAY

## Courage Requires Faith
### Read 1 Samuel 17

A friend invited me to hear him share his testimony at a church. He's a good guy, and wanted to make an impact, but he practically bragged about how well he was going to do.

Let me tell you, when he saw the crowd and heard the applause after being introduced, he froze. He could hardly get a word out. He later told me it was like his heart had jumped into his throat. The problem was, he was walking by sight, not faith.

You must understand that faith is not based on what's gathered through your senses—your nose, eyes, ears, mind, and hands. Faith kicks in when you take in that information but then pray for God's counsel about what to do. Faith allows the Holy Spirit to make decisions.

God instructs us to walk by faith and not by sight (2 Corinthians 5:7), but the Israelites must have skipped school that day, because they froze at the sight of Goliath. It didn't help when they heard him yell and curse their God for forty days. David, on the other hand, must have thought of his fellow Israelites: "What are these chumps scared of?" He ignored Goliath's threats and immediately believed by faith that he could—and would—kill the giant.

When you confront the giants of your life, do you listen to your fears or do you take courage in God? What problems or challenges do you face today that require the courage of David to defeat them? Even when things look impossible—when you have no friends to help you, no money in the bank, no idea where to turn—God can make it happen.

*With men this is impossible, but with God all things are possible.* —Matthew 19:26

## Interaction

What is the biggest obstacle that your senses say you cannot overcome but your faith says you can? Write it down and begin to pray for that giant-killer courage.

## Prayer

*Dear Lord, thank you for your Word. My prayer today is that what I see, hear, think, or feel would never discourage me. I pray that, by faith, I would take on all the challenges you set before me. I know from 2 Corinthians 10:5 that I need to bring every thought into captivity to the obedience of Christ. I pray that I would have faith to be a courageous, bad-to-the-bone giant-killer like David. In Jesus' name I pray, Amen.*

## Memory Verse

"Have I not commanded you? Be strong and of good courage; do not be afraid, nor be dismayed, for the Lord your God is with you wherever you go."

Joshua 1:9

# THURSDAY

## Courage Is Original

### Read 1 Samuel 17:38–50

During one of my son's soccer practices, we had each player dribble the ball to the left, fake right, then go left again. All the kids really got into the drill, except one. For some reason, Tony held back. He didn't even want to do it until we practically begged him. Tony usually loved to practice, so afterward I asked him what was up.

"I wanted to do it a different way," he said shyly, "but I thought that I'd get in trouble or that everyone would laugh at me."

"Oh, Tony. You should have told me," I said. "Next time, I want you to show us what you can do."

It takes courage to be original, especially if it means following God's way rather than the world's. In today's reading, Saul gave David all the standard tools necessary for battle.

*So Saul clothed David with his armor, and he put a bronze helmet on his head; he also clothed him with a coat of mail. David fastened his sword to his armor, and he tried to walk, for he had not tested them. . . .*

*—1 Samuel 17:38–39*

David had something else in mind. Rather than wear armor that was chosen out of fear, he decided to trust God.

*And David said to Saul, "I cannot walk with these, for I have not tested them." Then he took his staff in his hand; and he chose for himself five smooth stones from the brook, and put them in a shepherd's bag, in a pouch which he had, and his sling was in his hand. And he drew near to the Philistine.*

*—verses 39–40*

David didn't need armor to whup the giant. God would protect him. All David needed was incredible courage to be original—to go against worldly wisdom and instead do things God's way.

*"For My thoughts are not your thoughts, nor are your ways My ways," says the Lord. "For as the heavens are higher than the earth, so are My ways higher than your ways, and My thoughts than your thoughts."*

*—Isaiah 55:8–9*

It takes courage to accept and develop your God-given originality. It takes courage to resist sinful ways—to avoid alcohol when so-called friends want you to drink, to tell the truth when someone wants you to lie, to "keep it real" in the midst of phoniness. Like everyone else, you will feel fear at times when you go against the norm. But through prayer, God will help you become a courageous and original giant-killer.

## Interaction

Do you have an idea for doing something for God but are afraid of failing or being rejected because it is somehow different? God is the God of originality and creativity. Allow Him to challenge you to be the person He created, not what others want to create.

## Prayer

*Dear Lord, thank you for your Word. My prayer today is that I will never let fear prevent me from being my original self. I realize that you made me different from every person in the world. I must allow you—and you only—to mold and shape me into the person you designed me to be. I know now that it requires originality to be a courageous, bad-to-the-bone giant-killer like David. In Jesus' name I pray, Amen.*

## Memory Verse

"Have I not commanded you? Be strong and of good courage; do not be afraid, nor be dismayed, for the Lord your God is with you wherever you go."

Joshua 1:9

# FRIDAY

## Giant-Killers Remember

### Read 1 Samuel 17:20–37

Does it seem like every time you try to do something good, you get nothing but resistance? People or circumstances are against you? Someone says you can't or you won't?

With opposition like that, it's easy to doubt yourself. Just ask David, who had to dodge many obstacles in order to fight Goliath. First, King Saul told David he was too young. After all, Israel's entire army feared Goliath. Then David's brothers told him to go home and mind his own business.

Where did David get the strength to fight this giant? Well, it helped that David remembered all that God had done for him in the past.

*Your servant used to keep his father's sheep, and when a lion or a bear came and took a lamb out of the flock, I went out after it and struck it, and delivered the lamb from its mouth; and when it arose against me, I caught it by its beard, and struck and killed it. Your servant has killed both lion and bear; and this uncircumcised Philistine will be like one of them, seeing he has defied the armies of the living God.*

*—1 Samuel 17:34–36*

David continued,

*The Lord, who delivered me from the paw of the lion and from the paw of the bear, He will deliver me from the hand of this Philistine.*

*—verse 37*

Basically, David was saying, "I can't lose with the stuff I use." And in return, Saul let David go, knowing full well that if God had watched

39

over David in the past, He would surely fight David's battles in the future.

Everyone has stories of God's power and faithfulness, where God has helped beyond imagination. Maybe it was helping you finish a nasty assignment at school. Or maybe it was providing a friend or a job when you needed one. It's not always easy to recognize God's work, but He's there. When you face obstacles, remind yourself that God would not have brought you this far only to leave you high and dry.

## Interaction

Take a moment to write down a few situations in which God delivered you from the paw of a lion and a bear. Maybe there were even times when He rescued you from certain injury or death. Then ask yourself, why would He do that? Because He has plans for you.

## Prayer

*Dear Lord, thank you for your Word. My prayer today is that I will always remember what you have done for me. I know that I would not be here today if it had not been for your love and faithfulness in my life. Please continue to make your miracles plain to me and let me never forget that if you are for me, no one can be against me (Romans 8:31). I have nothing to fear when you send me to fight the giants of my life. May my memory help me grow into a courageous, bad-to-the-bone giant-killer like David. In Jesus' name I pray, Amen.*

## Memory Verse

"Have I not commanded you? Be strong and of good courage; do not be afraid, nor be dismayed, for the Lord your God is with you wherever you go."

Joshua 1:9

# WEEKEND WARRIOR
## Jehoiachin
### Read 2 Kings 24

On weekends, there's a big temptation to live it up and party, which leads to a second temptation: to forget your commitment to God. Satan's a pro at convincing people that they deserve time to have fun—his kind of fun. He'll tell you to forget about being a pure and straight kid. *It won't hurt to bend the rules for just one night*, Satan says.

Satan lies. God does not. And although our God is a forgiving God, today's reading shows that we pay for our sins.

Jehoiachin was eighteen and had it all. As the king of Israel he had power, money, women, and over seven thousand mighty fighting men.

*Jehoiachin was eighteen years old when he became king, and he reigned in Jerusalem three months. His mother's name was Nehushta the daughter of Elnathan of Jerusalem. And he did evil in the sight of the Lord, according to all that his father had done. At that time the servants of Nebuchadnezzar king of Babylon came up against Jerusalem, and the city was besieged.*
*—2 Kings 24:8–10*

Did you catch how long Jehoiachin's "fun" lasted before his world came crashing down? Three whole months. He was king for ninety days before his evil ways led to everything being captured by Nebuchadnezzar.

This weekend as you are faced with "living it up," remember that Satan is full of lies. He will tell you that you are invincible, indestructible. He will tell you that the fun will never end, but it always does. And God always prevails.

## Interaction

Write two ways Satan is trying to tempt you, and the two consequences you believe come along with those temptations.

## Prayer

*Dear God, thank you for your Word. I pray that every day, especially during the weekends, I will be faithful to my commitment to you. I thank you for Romans 6:23, which teaches, "The wages of sin is death, but the gift of God is eternal life in Christ Jesus our Lord." I pray that when I hear Satan encourage me to live it up, you will protect me and show me how to respond. May my decisions never cause me to turn my back on you. In Jesus' name I pray, Amen.*

# WEEKEND WARRIOR
## Jehoiachin
### Read 2 Kings 24

Have you ever wondered why God put certain stories in the Bible? Let's face it, God could have told us about countless people and miracles, but for some reason He chose the ones that are in the Bible. From some people in the Bible we learn what to do; from others, we learn what *not* to do.

In this weekend's reading, Jehoiachin gains fame for all the wrong reasons. He does evil in the eyes of the Lord and pays the price, as Galatians 6:7–8 warns:

> Do not be deceived, God is not mocked; for whatever a man sows, that he will also reap. For he who sows to his flesh will of the flesh reap corruption, but he who sows to the Spirit will of the Spirit reap everlasting life.

For Jehoiachin, he reaps the loss of his kingdom and is exiled to Babylon. That wasn't all, though. God wanted to make a lasting example of Jehoiachin. God could have simply put Jehoiachin's mug shot on the Old Testament's nightly news, and we'd probably never have even heard about him. Instead, God revealed Jehoiachin's failings in 2 Kings as a permanent warning to all of eternity.

Today, I want to challenge you to answer this: What kind of life are you living? Would God talk about you to encourage others or would He use your life as a warning about how not to live?

### Interaction

Write out the number one thing in your spiritual life that needs to change. Then pray for the desire to change it.

# Prayer

*Dear Lord, thank you for your Word. I pray that today and this upcoming week I can really surrender my old, sinful self to you. I don't want to have a bad reputation in heaven or on earth. I want my life to represent something good. I want to be an example to others, someone you can brag about as you did with David, Samuel, Mary, and so many others in the Bible. In Jesus' name I pray, Amen.*

## Be a Dreamer Like Joseph

Joseph was a seventeen-year-old dreamer who put his trust in God's promises. Not for a second did Joseph doubt God's calling for his life. He was to become ruler of Egypt. For Joseph, dreams weren't meaningless visions that appeared only when he slept. Dreams were promises that God would one day bring to reality.

God has given you the ability to dream; to see and achieve something bigger than you ever thought possible with your natural talents and abilities.

*Now to Him who is able to do exceedingly abundantly above all that we ask or think, according to the power that works in us, to Him be glory in the church by Christ Jesus to all generations, forever and ever. Amen.*

*—Ephesians 3:20–21*

But the question is, do you have what it takes to be a successful dreamer?

This week you will learn what it takes to become a dreamer—from the seventeen-year-old dreamer himself, Joseph. As you are reading and praying this week, the Holy Spirit will challenge you to be a bad-to-the-bone dreamer like Joseph, living in expectation that God's promises will come true. May God bless you as you study His Word this week.

# Memory Verse
# of the Week

Now to Him who is able to do exceedingly
abundantly above all that we ask or think,
according to the power that works in us,
to Him be glory.

EPHESIANS 3:20–21

# MONDAY

## Happy Dreaming

### Read Genesis 37

love to ask young people what they want to be when they grow up. You can only imagine what I've heard. I remember one guy who said he wanted to work in a factory. There's absolutely nothing wrong with that, but I sensed that he was taking a safe option.

"Why not own a factory?" I asked.

"Oh, I could never do that."

*I wonder how he knows what he can't do?* I thought.

It's not my place to decide what someone can or cannot do, but I do know beyond a shadow of a doubt what God can and cannot do. God can do anything. He is all-powerful and almighty in all things.

Have you ever caught yourself thinking, *I could never do that*? Have you ignored or put aside any dreams or aspirations because you thought they were impossible?

When God shares His plans for your life with you, it's normal to think, *I cannot do these in my own strength*. Guess what? You can't. But God is in the business of doing things that are impossible to man. And if you have faith in a BIG God to do BIG things, you can't help but get excited about His BIG dreams.

When God told Joseph through his dreams that he would rule over his family (Genesis 37:6–9), Joseph did not say, "God, that sounds good and all, but I think that's a bit aggressive. Don't you think I should just be one of the workers or field reps? Don't you think it might be a little unrealistic?" No, Joseph's response was "Wow, God, I'm gonna be DA MAN!" Joseph woke up and before doing anything else told his whole family about the dreams. *They should really be excited for me*, he must have thought.

If you think your dreams are unrealistic, ask yourself the following question: What is too big for God to do? Let me tell you the answer: Nothing! If you are going to dream, you might as well go for it and dream big. "For with God nothing will be impossible" (Luke 1:37).

No matter what you imagine or dream for your life, if it is God's will, He can and will make it happen, if you only believe.

## Interaction

List one dream of yours that you think is too big for God. Then list two reasons for your uncertainty. Surrender these to God in prayer.

## Prayer

*Dear Lord, thank you for your Word. My prayer today is that I will not be scared to dream big. I pray that I will never put a limit on what I believe you can or will do in my life. Please show me why I should not allow my reasons to discourage me. May I realize that my dreams only come true if they are yours to begin with and remain yours until the end. I pray that I can be a bad-to-the-bone dreamer like Joseph. In Jesus' name I pray, Amen.*

## Memory Verse

Now to Him who is able to do exceedingly abundantly above all that we ask or think, according to the power that works in us, to Him be glory.

Ephesians 3:20–21

# TUESDAY

## No Fear!

### Read Genesis 39–40

I was in the airport one day when a sixteen-year-old guy asked if he could shine my leather sneakers. They looked fine to me, so I decided to just talk with him.

I soon learned that he had barely completed junior high school before dropping out. He told me about his job, but I couldn't help wanting to know his dreams; if he even had a dream.

"What do you want to be when you grow up?" I asked. He thought a moment and shrugged his shoulders.

I told him about my ministry, then asked, "If I could guarantee success in whatever you try, what would you do? What would you try to achieve?" I could tell he thought it was a trick question, but then he surprised me with his answer:

"I'd become a Christian."

"Why do you say that?"

"Because . . . you can't fail with God?" he half asked, half said.

I gave him a big smile and found out that he knew enough about God to know that God never lets us down. God is always faithful in keeping His promises.

"God wants you to do big things with your life," I told the young man. "Don't be afraid of failing."

In today's reading, we see that Joseph is a young man who understood God's faithfulness. Joseph wasn't afraid of failure. Through his ups and downs, he always had God. Never at any point in his life did Joseph view himself as a failure.

What is your dream today? God wants to give you a vision. But you cannot be a dreamer like Joseph if you fear failure. You must believe that if God is the source of your dream, He will make sure it ends up the way He wants.

## Interaction

What would you love to try for God but worry that it might fail? Write it down under the words "No Fear," begin to pray, and go for it.

## Prayer

*Dear Lord, thank you for your Word. I pray that I will never limit what you can do in my life. I pray that I will never let fear influence my belief in your ability to complete your plan in my life. I pray that I will have no fear of failure when I set out to achieve my dreams. For in Romans 8:15, you teach, "For you did not receive the spirit of bondage again to fear, but you received the Spirit of adoption by whom we cry out, 'Abba, Father.' " Lord, make me into a bad-to-the-bone dreamer like Joseph. In Jesus' name I pray, Amen.*

## Memory Verse

Now to Him who is able to do exceedingly abundantly above all that we ask or think, according to the power that works in us, to Him be glory.

Ephesians 3:20–21

# WEDNESDAY

## Lazy?

### Read Genesis 41–42

Growing up, I used to love it when new kids moved into the neighborhood. You see, I was the best when it came time to hand out nicknames; nothing nasty, just a word that fit their style—something that described them.

Nothing's changed now that I have my own family. I'm always making up nicknames for our kids. I hate to say it, but our oldest daughter is definitely our lazy child. We don't go around calling her lazy, but she admits that she's always looking for a shortcut to hard work.

A good dreamer cannot afford to be lazy. As a matter of fact, a good dreamer should not even know how to spell *lazy*. Ecclesiastes 5:3 says, "A dream comes through much activity, and a fool's voice is known by his many words." Got that? Dreams require hard work.

Joseph's dream required an incredible amount of work and learning. He had to "handle his business" in the classroom, learning a foreign language and culture. He had to manage the food supply of the entire world by developing systems to stock and distribute the food. God was behind Joseph's dream, but a bad work ethic or lazy habits would have definitely prevented Joseph from fulfilling his dream.

## Interaction

When it comes to the dreams and goals that God has placed on your heart, write down two ways in which you are lazy. Then write down what you need to do to become a hard worker in these areas. Include in your prayer a commitment to overcome this laziness.

## Prayer

*Dear Lord, thank you for your Word. Thank you for showing us that we need to work hard to make dreams come true. I pray that you will show me how to avoid wasting time during the day on things that are not part of your plan for my life. I want to get the most out of my day as possible, and I know that what I achieve is directly related to my willingness to work. With hard work, I know that I can be a bad-to-the-bone dreamer like Joseph. In Jesus' name I pray, Amen.*

## Memory Verse

Now to Him who is able to do exceedingly abundantly above all that we ask or think, according to the power that works in us, to Him be glory.

Ephesians 3:20-21

# THURSDAY
## Price of a Dream
### Read Genesis 39:7–20

One of the most famous one-liners in sports is *No pain, No gain*. In many ways, this saying applies just as much to life outside the gym.

If you are going to accomplish important things in your life for God, be prepared to suffer to some degree. God prepared Joseph to be a great ruler by placing him in difficult situations. For instance, the Bible tells us that Joseph's brothers held a grudge against him.

> *Now Israel loved Joseph more than all his children, because he was the son of his old age. Also he made him a tunic of many colors. But when his brothers saw that their father loved him more than all his brothers, they hated him and could not speak peaceably to him.*
>
> *—Genesis 37:3–4*

Joseph's brothers took their anger to the next level when they tied him up and sold him into slavery. Imagine the rejection he felt having his own brothers turn on him. Then, as we see in today's reading, Joseph's troubles continued when he was thrown in jail, all because he was determined to stay sexually pure. Through it all, however, God's love for Joseph remained strong.

Don't underestimate God's ways of preparing you for His plan. Know, too, that Satan will be determined to destroy your hope and optimism for a bright future. You must decide how you will react to trials. What are you going to do when things don't go your way, when unexpected hard times come? How will you react when you are mistreated? Satan will use obstacles such as these to discourage you, but it is during trying times that

God wants you to trust Him more, so that you will be stronger in the end. It's the price you might have to pay—the price of a dream.

Joseph paid the price starting at age seventeen, and in the end became one of the most powerful men in the world. You are that teenager now. God is preparing you—yes, even through pain and suffering. Perhaps you've been rejected, like Joseph, by family members. Whatever the trial, God is preparing you for something bigger and better than you can imagine. You must believe and trust that He who began the dream in your heart will complete it in your life, even though sometimes you must pass through the valley of the shadow of death to make it happen (Psalm 23:4). Let the valley prepare you for what is on the other side.

## Interaction

Are you going through any trials, facing any challenges, at this time? I guarantee that if you pray and ask God for wisdom He will begin to reveal how He is using these difficult times to prepare you for something big— something you could never do on your own. Write down the trials in your life, followed by what you think God wants you to learn from them.

## Prayer

*Dear Lord, thank you for your Word. My prayer today is I that will realize that even bad times can be used to make my dreams come true. I pray for the wisdom to learn the lessons of life's hard times. I pray that I will always remember that you will get me through my problems and at the same time make me a stronger person. I pray that I could be a bad-to-the-bone dreamer like Joseph. In Jesus' name, Amen.*

## Memory Verse

Now to Him who is able to do exceedingly abundantly above all that we ask or think, according to the power that works in us, to Him be glory.

Ephesians 3:20–21

# FRIDAY
## Hit the Sack
### Read Genesis 40

I look forward to going to sleep every night, not only for the rest it provides but to have a dream. I've always been a dreamer. Whether I take a ten-minute nap or I'm out cold for the night, I have a vivid dream—sometimes even in four parts.

There are two kinds of dreams: dreams that come in the form of thoughts and images during sleep and dreams that represent major aims or goals that we want to accomplish. Either way, God can be the source of that dream. The tough part is figuring out what God is trying to tell us through dreams.

In the Scripture verses that we focus on today, God gives Joseph the ability to interpret the sleep-dreams of two fellow prisoners, the chief butler (called the chief cupbearer in some Bible translations) and the chief baker. The butler's dream represented good news: He would soon get his old job back from the pharaoh. The baker wasn't so fortunate. He was hanged three days later.

For Joseph, God placed in him an incredible dream—to become the ruler of Egypt and save many, many people, including his family, from certain death during the famine. In no way could Joseph achieve this dream without God. But Joseph trusted God and followed God's directions for his life.

Want to know God's dream for your life? You'll need to do three things.

First, go to sleep. I don't mean literally going to sleep, y'know, the mouth-wide-open-snoring-on-the-pillow kind of sleep. No! What I mean is that you need to get away where it is quiet and listen to God—a place where you can focus on God's voice and His direction for your life.

Second, write down what you sense God is telling you. Habakkuk 2:2–3 says, "Then the Lord answered me and said: 'Write the vision and make it plain on tablets, that he may run who reads it. For the vision is yet for an appointed time; but at the end it will speak, and it will not lie. Though it tarries, wait for it; because it will surely come, it will not tarry.' " Writing down your dreams will help you to understand them.

Third, start pursuing your dream. Begin with very simple steps, working out the details. To get more direction and help in developing your ideas, talk with your parents and/or an adult you trust who can possibly be your mentor. Let people know about your dreams, your aspirations, and God will honor your faith. He will open and close the right doors of opportunity as you proceed by faith.

## Interaction

Write down a dream that God has placed on your heart; something you can only accomplish with God's help. Then make a commitment to begin to make it happen.

## Prayer

*Dear Lord, thank you for your Word. My prayer today is I that would be more thoughtful when I consider the dreams you put on my heart. May I remember to listen to you and write down what you say, then by faith begin to walk in the path you set before me. Faith is proven by action, so I must act on my dreams and start to become a bad-to-the-bone dreamer like Joseph. In Jesus' name I pray, Amen.*

## Memory Verse

Now to Him who is able to do exceedingly abundantly above all that we ask or think, according to the power that works in us, to Him be glory.

Ephesians 3:20–21

# WEEKEND WARRIOR
## Joseph
### Read Genesis 37:3–4

t's the weekend, but I still want to look at Joseph's life and what we can learn from him. I've got to admit, though, I didn't like Joseph at first. To me, he was a spoiled brat. Of the twelve sons, Joseph clearly was his dad's favorite.

*Now Israel loved Joseph more than all his children, because he was the son of his old age. Also he made him a tunic of many colors. But when his brothers saw that their father loved him more than all his brothers, they hated him and could not speak peaceably to him.*

*—Genesis 37:3–4*

I'm sure you know someone who's spoiled—a rich friend or, who knows, maybe even your own brother or sister. They seem to get anything and everything they ask for. Not only is this irritating to the rest of us, it can hurt. *Why is she so popular? Why does he get the breaks? God must love them more than me.*

Well, there's good news for you and me. God doesn't show any favoritism. We might not have as much stuff as the next guy or look like a supermodel, but God loves us more than we even know. Best of all, His love is unconditional, which is more than you can say about most people. God wants to bless you more than you can handle.

*For I know the thoughts that I think toward you, says the Lord, thoughts of peace and not of evil, to give you a future and a hope.*

*—Jeremiah 29:11*

To experience God's dreams for you—His big plans for you—you have to believe deep in your heart that He doesn't want to harm you. God wants to bless you and use you more than you can ask or imagine. If you don't believe that, it will be impossible to pursue the vision God places in your heart. If you doubt God you cannot please God. The Bible says that without faith it is impossible to please God (Hebrews 11:6), and faith and doubt cannot dwell together.

My challenge to you is to realize that God wants to spoil you, not in a worldly sense, but spiritually. This weekend, stop and spend time alone with God. Receive His encouragement and vision for your life. And when God gives you that vision, believe and accept it because He loves you more than you know.

## Interaction

Spend one hour today with a pen and a piece of paper and ask God to give you a vision—a dream for your life. No matter how big it is, write it down.

## Prayer

*Dear Lord, thank you for your Word. Thank you for loving me more than I love myself. I pray that you would show me how much you love me. Give me the faith to receive that love, to believe that you indeed want to spoil me with spiritual growth. I know that you want me to live by faith (Romans 1:17), so I ask for the desire to read my Bible in order to grow my faith and become a successful, bad-to-the-bone dreamer like Joseph. In Jesus' name, Amen.*

# WEEKEND WARRIOR
## Joseph
### Read Genesis 37:1–28

recently enjoyed a two-week tour of Israel. It was the chance of a lifetime to visit the places we read about in the Bible, to see where Jesus walked, taught, died, and rose again. Because today's landscape is drastically different than biblical times, the tour guides often told us to imagine what a particular hill or field would look like without the buildings there now.

While we were visiting a shepherd's field in Bethlehem, a young boy walking by with his fifty or so sheep made me think, *That could be what David looked like; how he cared for his sheep.* Before long, I was having similar thoughts about practically every young person we encountered. *Did Esther look like her? Is that how Joseph looked?*

Joseph was seventeen when he was sold for about a half pound of silver to the Ishmaelites. For the next thirteen years he was a slave in Egypt. All along, though, God had a plan that Joseph would do mighty things for Him.

Do you believe that God can use *you* to do awesome things, things like preaching in your school, praying for your friends' salvation, being a leader, displaying godly courage, maximizing your God-given talents? Why can't God use you to revolutionize the world? He can! As long as you have the faith to believe.

Joseph, Daniel, Rebekah, and other bad-to-the-bone teenagers in the Bible received a command from God to do something that was impossible by their natural abilities. But with God's help, they did it.

God has called you in the same way. Hold on to God and He will take you far. You will do things you never dreamed possible.

I challenge you to reach out to God, asking Him to use you like He used the Bible heroes featured in this devotional. Be a preacher, a teacher, a prayer warrior, a servant, a giant-killer, a king, a leader. God only knows what you are capable of.

## Interaction

If you could be one young person from the Bible, who would you choose and why? Write down what you admire about this person and what you can do to be more like him or her.

## Prayer

*Dear Lord, thank you for your Word today. I pray that I will begin to be transformed into a modern-day Bible hero, a Christian who you can trust to carry out a major plan for your kingdom. Please bless me with the wisdom, courage, and vision that is needed to be a man/woman of God now in my teenage years. Please confirm this blessing by sending an adult into my life who will encourage and teach me how to live for you. In Jesus' name I pray, Amen.*

# WEEK 4

## Be Worthy Like Esther

Esther entered the biggest beauty contest ever. The winner would be queen of an entire country. For twelve months she received special beauty treatments, and in the end she won. Esther knew she was FINE.

To many people, this moment might seem like the beginning of Esther's life on easy street. In reality, though, it led to the biggest test of her life.

Shortly after Esther's dream had come true, she found herself in a dangerous position. All the Jews were going to be killed unless she stepped forward and confronted the king. She had two choices: put her crown—and her life—on the line by revealing the evil plan and admitting that she was a Jew; or, stay quiet and hide her Jewish heritage, letting her fellow Jews die. Esther knew she owed her life to God. He had chosen her for a special job at a special time, and in return, she risked everything for Him. She wanted to prove she was worthy of God's love.

This week the Holy Spirit will challenge you to be bad-to-the-bone worthy like Esther. May God bless you as you study His Word this week.

# Memory Verse
# of the Week

For we are His workmanship, created in
Christ Jesus for good works, which God
prepared beforehand that we should
walk in them.

EPHESIANS 2:10

# MONDAY

## Use It Or Lose It

### Read Esther 5–6

I n my fourth year with the San Diego Chargers, we drafted a defensive player named Richard who had more physical talent than any other lineman I had seen. Not only was he one of the biggest guys on the team but he was as fast as a defensive back. Richard was as strong as they come. He could throw three-hundred-pound men around with one arm. He was simply amazing, except for one shortfall—he never worked out. With all his natural strength, he didn't think it was necessary. Besides, until the NFL he had always been the biggest, baddest player on the field. All he had to do was show up and kick some butt.

Richard never worked out, nor did he study game film. Many people don't realize that pro football players prepare for upcoming games by studying films of the opposition for at least two or three hours each day. Really dedicated players take films home to further analyze the other team's strategies and strengths and weaknesses.

Let me tell you, Richard was in for a big surprise now that he was playing in the big time. There were plenty of strong, fast guys in the league to challenge him. In our first game, Richard lined up against someone who wasn't as big or strong as Richard, but the guy was smart. He used and abused Richard like he was stealing candy from a child.

Richard didn't realize that he had a responsibility to develop and use his natural talents to the best of his ability. The same goes for the rest of us. The only way to show God that you respect and honor the talents He has given you is to grow and use those talents as He would want them. God gave you your talents for a specific purpose.

The Lord tells us that to whom much is given, much is required (Luke 12:48). Esther was given loads of beauty and a great opportunity, but then she was asked to give it all up. She had the looks, the smile, the hair, and the walk, but more importantly, she approached life from God's perspective. She understood that everything about her belonged to God and it was her responsibility to be ready whenever He called on her.

## Interaction

What is God requiring of you to do with the talents and gifts He has given you?

## Prayer

*Dear Lord, thank you for your Word today. I pray that I will be a good steward over the talents you have given me. I pray that I will place great worth in your plan for my life and that I will appreciate what you have called me to do. I pray that I will be able to identify my bad-to-the-bone worth to you just like Esther did. In Jesus' name I pray, Amen.*

## Memory Verse

For we are His workmanship, created in Christ Jesus for good works, which God prepared beforehand that we should walk in them.

Ephesians 2:10

# TUESDAY

## Made for Such a Time as This

### Read Esther 4

Lots of things in this world are beyond my understanding. Sometimes I catch myself wondering why some people seem to be blessed while others have a difficult life. Some people are gifted in sports; others excel in school. Some people are mechanically inclined, while others have amazing speaking skills or incredible personalities.

In the natural world, these traits have little lasting value. Our bodies die and go into the ground. But in the spiritual world, it's totally different.

I have come to realize that God has a specific use for everyone—if only we will let Him use us. God places people in specific places at specific times for specific reasons beyond what we could ever know.

*For we are His workmanship, created in Christ Jesus for good works, which God prepared beforehand that we should walk in them.*

*—Ephesians 2:10*

Your talents and abilities will always match perfectly the circumstances God creates for you. Whether your talents are in sports, academics, making friends, or whatever, God has a plan.

We must always look for opportunities to use our God-given talents. Esther could have taken it easy and said, "Don't hate me because I'm beautiful." Instead, she realized that she had won the beauty contest so that she could be used to save her people. As Mordecai said, God had made her beautiful—for such a time as this (Esther 4:14).

Take a second and think about your life. Why has God placed you in your community, in your school, in your family, in the circumstances that surround you? Our value or worth to God is directly connected but not limited to our ability to represent Him in our lives every day. That's what motivated Esther.

## Interaction

Why do you think God created you at this time? Has anyone ever said God would use you in a specific way? Write down at least one reason why you think God made you. Share this with someone who can pray with you about it.

## Prayer

*Dear Lord, thank you for your Word. I pray that I could by faith acknowledge that there is a reason you have made me; there is a purpose for my life. You have chosen me at this time in this place to be used in a special way—which only you could design. I pray that I can trust that one day you will reveal my purpose so that I may have a stronger sense of my bad-to-the-bone worth like Esther. In Jesus' name I pray, Amen.*

## Memory Verse

For we are His workmanship, created in Christ Jesus for good works, which God prepared beforehand that we should walk in them.

Ephesians 2:10

# WEDNESDAY

## I Am Beautiful!

### Read Esther 2

I grew up with two brothers and two sisters. All of us shared the same bathroom, which made waiting outside the door an all-too-common occurrence. My oldest sister was the bathroom queen. Sometimes she spent five hours in there just working on her face. Okay, maybe not five hours, but it was a whole lot longer than I spent on my face. I barely washed mine. She'd put on foundation, eyeliner, mascara, lipstick, and on and on. To tell you the truth, I really don't know what she did in there, I just know it took a long time.

Fortunately, our outward beauty doesn't mean a thing in the eyes of the Lord. He doesn't care how we look.

*". . . The Lord does not see as man sees; for man looks at the outward appearance, but the Lord looks at the heart."*
—*1 Samuel 16:7*

When you accept Jesus as your Savior, He places into your heart His Holy Spirit, along with His righteousness, His holiness, and His love. God gives you His attributes—the qualities that make up your godly worth. You won't see God's gifts by looking in a mirror, but they should be evident to others by how you act, how much you reflect the love of Christ.

Esther was bad-to-the-bone beautiful. But her worth did not come from her appearance. It came from the godly qualities within her. Inner strength and devotion last longer than outer beauty.

*For he is not a Jew who is one outwardly, nor is circumcision that which is outward in the flesh; but he is a Jew who is one inwardly; and circumcision is that of the heart, in the Spirit, not in the*

*letter; whose praise is not from men but from God.*
*—Romans 2:28–29*

*Do not let your adornment be merely outward—arranging the hair, wearing gold, or putting on fine apparel, rather let it be the hidden person of the heart, with the incorruptible beauty of a gentle and quiet spirit, which is very precious in the sight of God.*
*—1 Peter 3:3–4*

*Therefore we do not lose heart. Even though our outward man is perishing, yet the inward man is being renewed day by day.*
*—2 Corinthians 4:16*

## Interaction

List as many of your God-given attributes as you can and note which ones you think you display on a regular basis. Are there attributes that need developing? Each day of this week pick one to work on.

## Prayer

*Dear Lord, thank you for your Word. Thank you that the most valuable attributes I have are not outward, but inward. They are wrapped in the character traits you have given me. I pray that I will identify with them so much that they will change the way I act. I pray that I will adopt them into my everyday life so that I can experience a biblical sense of bad-to-the-bone worth like Esther. In Jesus' name I pray, Amen.*

## Memory Verse

For we are His workmanship, created in Christ Jesus for good works, which God prepared beforehand that we should walk in them.

Ephesians 2:10

# THURSDAY

## What's In a Name?

### Read Esther 1

While reading the Bible, I especially notice names of people that have special meanings. Did you know that Adam means earth? Esther was derived from the name Star. We all know what a star is, but the dictionary adds some detail, saying it is a gaseous object in space that emits light. Thus, Esther's name implies that the light or righteousness of Christ shines in her.

Do you know if your name has a special meaning? I can tell you what your spiritual name *Christian* means: little Christ. That's right, Christian means little Christ. No matter who you become in life, you will always have the label "little Christ." Having this name, we are called to act like Christ—a pretty heavy responsibility when you consider what Jesus did for us.

If Jesus suffered and died so that you could be called a Christian, the question you must ask yourself is: How far are you willing to go to match that level of sacrifice? What are you willing to surrender or sacrifice in order to enjoy the abundant life Jesus has for you?

*"For whoever desires to save his life will lose it, but whoever loses his life for My sake and the gospel's will save it."* —Mark 8:35

Stars in the sky eventually burn out and fade away. But be a star like Esther and the light of the Lord will shine constantly in your life. Begin by accepting that with the Christian name comes the history of Jesus' life and sacrifice—all so that you could be forgiven and live a life worthy of repentance. Take great pride in what God has given in His Spirit and what He has called you to do with your life.

## Interaction

A few questions to consider:

What do you think God expects from you as a Christian? ("A new commandment I give to you, that you love one another; as I have loved you, that you also love one another." John 13:34)

What responsibility comes with the name *Christian*? ("Not everyone who says to Me, 'Lord, Lord,' shall enter the kingdom of heaven, but he who does the will of My Father in heaven." Matthew 7:21)

What commitment does God make to people who take His name? ("I am the good shepherd. The good shepherd gives His life for the sheep." John 10:11)

## Prayer

*Dear Lord, thank you for your Word. I pray that today I can keep in mind that the name you have given me has serious meaning. I must be a little Christ today. I must talk, act, love, and forgive like you today. I pray that I would not bring shame to your name. I pray that my bad-to-the-bone worth will be displayed in my actions through unselfish obedience. In Jesus' name I pray, Amen.*

## Memory Verse

For we are His workmanship, created in Christ Jesus for good works, which God prepared beforehand that we should walk in them.

Ephesians 2:10

# FRIDAY

# Commitment to Her People

### Read Esther 4–7

Every Sunday countless people attend a church somewhere in the world. Sadly, for many people, that's the only time they connect with fellow believers. Their commitment to other people of faith is minimal at best.

Esther could have taken on the same attitude. When Haman threatened to kill the Jews, Esther could have looked out only for herself and saved her pretty head. Even her adopted father, Mordecai, warned, "Do not think in your heart that you will escape in the king's palace any more than all the other Jews" (Esther 4:13).

No, Esther threw caution to the wind. Her undeniable connection with her people led her to ask the king, "If I have found favor in your sight, O king, and if it pleases the king, let my life be given me at my petition, and my people at my request" (Esther 7:3). And the king honored Esther's request.

When Jesus saved our lives, it meant sacrificing His own life so that our sinful ways would no longer make us God's enemy: "God demonstrates His own love toward us, in that while we were still sinners, Christ died for us" (Romans 5:8).

How far are *you* willing to go for those who call on the name of Jesus? Better yet, how far are you willing to go to help those who don't call on the name of the Lord? Are you willing to be an example and source of encouragement to nonbelievers?

## Interaction

When the day is over, be prepared to write down the instances in which you did something solely to help someone in their faith.

## Prayer

*Dear Lord, thank you for your Word. I pray today that I can be used to help and encourage someone else today. I pray that I will live according to Philippians 2:4–7, which says, "Let each of you look out not only for his own interests, but also for the interests of others. Let this mind be in you which was also in Christ Jesus, who, being in the form of God, did not consider it robbery to be equal with God, but made Himself of no reputation, taking the form of a bondservant, and coming in the likeness of men." May these words from the apostle Paul be on my mind all day. May I live a worthy, bad-to-the-bone life like Esther. In Jesus' name I pray, Amen.*

## Memory Verse

For we are His workmanship, created in Christ Jesus for good works, which God prepared beforehand that we should walk in them.

Ephesians 2:10

# WEEKEND WARRIOR
## Abishag
### Read 1 Kings 1:1–4

I am privileged to travel and speak in schools all over the country. Several years ago I was in Philadelphia for a week when I saw a newspaper story about three hundred local teenagers who had donated blood. *Cool,* I thought to myself. *These are kids who really want to help others.* But then I read on. It turned out that during the standard blood screening process, ninety of the three hundred kids were found to be HIV positive. Nearly one in three suddenly received a death sentence—all because they had engaged in activity they thought was harmless. They shared needles or had sex (perhaps even believing that they could protect themselves with a condom). These kids were going to die because of their mistake.

In today's Bible reading, it is very important to note that there was no sexual contact between Abishag and David, nor was there any evil intent. For one thing, Abishag wasn't about to mess around. She was not that kind of girl. She had simply been asked to lie beside the aging David to keep him warm. And David, we can imagine, obviously respected the girl enough to not take advantage of the situation.

Still, Satan has a way of turning innocent relationships into evil. In no time flat he can turn an innocent hug into a sensual hug, an innocent kiss into a sensual kiss. He has a way of perverting everything that God has meant for good. He'll tell you that all you need is a relationship; get a great-looking person on your arm and you'll be happy. But this is not true. It goes against God's wishes.

*Flee also youthful lusts; but pursue righteousness, faith, love, peace with those who call on the Lord out of a pure heart.*
—*2 Timothy 2:22*

The Bible says that we shouldn't trust our body and its sinful ways (Romans 6:12) or even trust other people (Psalm 146:3–4). Instead, we should trust only Jesus Christ. He alone provides true life—abundant and eternal. This weekend, you may have an opportunity to spend innocent time with a companion. Be careful that it stays that way. Keep your relationships clean and simple. The Bible clearly says that immoral and impure persons will not inherit the kingdom of God (Ephesians 5:5).

## Interaction

Write down some ways the Devil can turn an innocent relationship into a sinful one. List specific ways you can avoid Satan's traps this weekend and beyond.

## Prayer

*Dear Lord, thank you for your Word. Thank you for the friends you have given me—the young men or women that I respect and love as friends. I thank you for teaching me how to relate to people of the opposite sex, and I pray that you will help me treat them with respect and not allow the Devil to turn an innocent relationship into a sinful one. I pray that I will be pure this weekend and beyond. In Jesus' name, Amen.*

# WEEKEND WARRIOR
## Abishag
### Read 1 Kings 1:1–4

When I was nineteen I had a summer job in Brooklyn, New York, as inspector of a construction site. It happened to be in a Puerto Rican neighborhood filled with little kids.

Almost every day I saw a certain five-year-old girl, Jaci. She was the cutest little girl, with big brown eyes and long hair. From the moment I met Jaci, she had me wrapped around her finger. She'd ask me in her sweet way to do things for her. I became her buddy, and she knew how to get me to do whatever she wanted. She'd call out to me from a block away and I'd run to receive her orders. I was a mess.

The thing about little girls is that they become grown-up girls. And some learn how to abuse their charms to get guys. Girls' weapons increase as their bodies and personalities develop. The same is true for boys as they grow up. They learn how to seduce girls and get them to do things that are sinful.

In this weekend's Bible reading, the men of Israel searched for a young woman to lie with King David to keep him warm. They had specific qualifications:

> *"Let a young woman, a virgin, be sought for our lord the king, and let her stand before the king, and let her care for him; and let her lie in your bosom, that our lord the king may be warm."*
> —*1 Kings 1:2*

The Devil is a master at copying what God does. Because Satan can't create on his own, he takes and perverts God's creation. Abishag was sought to keep David *alive*; the Devil will seek young, beautiful women and men to *tempt and destroy* other people.

If God has given you a jammin' smile, charming personality, a great body, don't allow the Devil to use it for evil. I promise that he is looking for someone just like you, someone through whom he can bring death. Whether this weekend or sometime down the road, Satan will send opportunity your way. He will bring people into your life who think they need a pretty face to keep them alive or keep them happy. It is your responsibility not to allow the Devil to implement his plan through you. Be careful this weekend and only allow God to use you for good.

## Interaction

It is important to prepare for temptation before it comes. Write down the most tempting situation you think you will face this weekend, then list how you are going to avoid sinning.

## Prayer

*Dear Lord, thank you for your Word. I pray that I would not be tricked into being used for evil by Satan. Please give me the discernment and strength to flee youthful lust. In Jesus' name I pray, Amen.*

WEEK 5

# Be About Your Father's Business Like Jesus

Jesus was God in the flesh, born to an earthly mother. He grew up like all other children, with brothers and sisters, a mom and dad. The Bible contains many, many stories about Jesus' adult ministry, but there is only one story from his youth. When Jesus was twelve, he found himself talking with adults in the temple about adult things. He was taking care of His "Father's business."

By growing in the grace and knowledge of the Lord this week, the Holy Spirit will challenge you to be about your Father's business like Jesus. May God bless you as you study His Word this week.

# Memory Verse
# of the Week

"Not everyone who says to Me, 'Lord, Lord,'
shall enter the kingdom of heaven, but he
who does the will of My Father in heaven."

MATTHEW 7:21

# MONDAY

## Godly Boy Jesus

### Read Luke 2:39–50

I lead two Sunday night services at my church in San Diego. The first service attracts mostly thirty- to forty-year-olds. The second service gets a younger, livelier crowd—mostly high school- and college-aged people, rebels for God who come ready to worship and have fun.

Some people think that because the young people are lively and wild, they are less mature. But I wholeheartedly disagree. Grown-up does not mean mature.

The Bible often compares believers or some aspect of our faith with a branch, vine, or seed. These metaphors or word pictures talk about maturity as being in a healthy growing process. For example, with water and good soil, a seed will sprout and grow toward the sun. During every moment of this process it is considered a mature plant. Whether one month old or ten years old, if it is healthy and growing, it is mature.

Jesus went through a growth process, and yet He was spiritually mature even at a young age: "The Child grew and became strong in spirit, filled with wisdom; and the grace of God was upon Him" (Luke 2:40).

You, too, can be spiritually mature at your age. The key question is, Are you growing?

- ✗ Are you acting like the branches in John 5:15, depending solely on Jesus the vine for wisdom, direction, and grace?
- ✗ Are you reading the Bible and growing your mustard seed of faith? (Matthew 17:20; Luke 17:6)
- ✗ Are you "like a tree planted by the rivers of water, that brings forth its fruit in its season, whose leaf also shall not wither"? (Psalm 1:3)

In order to be about your Father's business like Jesus, you must be growing in the grace and knowledge of the Lord himself.

## Interaction

One sign of maturity is the lack of bad habits. Check how well you are growing and maturing by listing any bad habits that you no longer do. Then choose a bad habit that you still need to beat down. Focus all of your prayers, Bible reading, and effort on changing this bad habit into a good one.

## Prayer

*Dear Lord, thank you for your Word. My prayer today is that I would continue to grow in the grace and knowledge of Jesus Christ. Give me a hunger and thirst for godly things. May I wake up each morning with a desire to pray and read my Bible. Grant me a supernatural urge to stop making the same mistakes over and over again. Please, God, give me the desire to be a bad-to-the-bone believer and be about your business like Jesus. In Jesus' name I pray, Amen.*

## Memory Verse

"Not everyone who says to Me, 'Lord, Lord,' shall enter the kingdom of heaven, but he who does the will of My Father in heaven."

Matthew 7:21

# TUESDAY

## Po' Boy

### Read Luke 2:21–38

Think you've got it rough? A while back I spoke at a fundraiser for young people on skid row. You should have heard their stories and seen where they lived. If they weren't living on the street, they lived in a building packed with "apartments" the size of an average bedroom—about twelve feet by twelve feet. Everyone in the building shared a bathroom; everyone lived in the midst of roaches, rats, and horrible smells.

The kids came from all over, but each had an amazingly similar story. Their parents, if they were in the picture at all, were usually drug addicts. Many of the kids talked about when they were younger and came home to an empty apartment because their parents had been evicted. Most had dropped out of school after eighth grade, and now they were barely existing.

It was at this fundraiser that God broke my heart—twice. The first time was simply seeing where the kids lived. The second time was when they started to sing, "I have the joy, joy, joy, joy down in my heart . . . down in my heart to stay." They followed with R. Kelly's song from *Space Jam* that includes the words "I believe I can fly, I believe I can touch the sky, I think about it every night and day, spread my wings and fly away." Think about it, these kids were living on the street or in one-room apartments, but their ability and desire to dream lived on. They had not given up.

I began to cry. All I could think about was their horrible living conditions; conditions that would certainly take their lives and hope if not for Jesus.

Jesus himself was born into a poor family dealing with tough circumstances. After His birth, Jesus' family had to flee the country because King Herod had issued a contract on His life.

Even as a poor and marked child, Jesus found the time and energy to be about His Father's business. Due to His poverty, Jesus didn't have anything to lose, which was His attitude toward life and ministry. He lived as though He had nothing to lose. His poverty and dangerous life had no effect on His ability to obey His Father in heaven.

Never let the conditions in this world be your excuse for any lack of commitment and productivity in the spiritual world. To spread the Gospel you don't need lots of money, fancy clothes, or a great speaking ability. No earthly circumstances can hold you hostage and prevent you from accessing God through prayer and obedience. Don't let poverty or tough situations keep you from enjoying your spiritual riches.

## Interaction

Are you mad at God for any reason? If so, are you holding that against Him? Have your complaints against God become an excuse for not doing His work? Write down any complaints you have against God, then cross them out, committing to never allow Satan to use them to distract you again from being about your Father's business.

## Prayer

*Dear Lord, thank you for your Word. My prayer today is that I would never allow poverty or difficult conditions to be an excuse for my lack of spiritual obedience. I realize that Jesus was a poor child and often had no place to live, but this never prevented Him from praying and being obedient. May I always be a bad-to-the-bone believer and be about my Father's business like Jesus, no matter how uncomfortable my circumstances. In Jesus' name I pray, Amen.*

## Memory Verse

"Not everyone who says to Me, 'Lord, Lord,' shall enter the kingdom of heaven, but he who does the will of My Father in heaven."

Matthew 7:21

# WEDNESDAY

## Respect Your Parents

### Read Luke 2:41–52

I meet many young people who seem to be truly seeking God. Their prayers come from the Holy Spirit. They run campus ministries, oversee discipleship groups, lead worship services, sing in church choirs.

Unfortunately, I have learned that not everyone is as they appear. Too often I've been impressed by someone only to be sadly surprised to hear the other side of their story from their parents. These same young people who appeared to be walking with God were living a double life. They put on a good show, but at home they were anything but godly.

Jesus was not like that. His life was consistent in everything. In today's Bible reading, we see that at the age of twelve, Jesus hung out in the temple and peppered the rabbis with questions while amazing them with his own understanding and answers. Jesus was the Son of God—His parents would eventually bow their knee to Him like all of us—yet "He went down with them and came to Nazareth, and was [obedient] to them" (Luke 2:51).

Are you a different person at home than at church? If I asked your pastor and parents about you, would I get two different stories? Are you living a double life? Do you respect your parents as much as your coach, teachers, or youth pastor? No matter how old you are or how much you know, you must always show respect for your parents. Even if they are not believers, your unconditional love and respect for them can be your strongest witness. The fifth commandment says,

*Honor your father and your mother, that your days may be long upon the land which the Lord your God is giving you.*
*—Exodus 20:12*

By the way, did you know that this is the only commandment that includes a promise from God? Honor your parents, and God will bless the quality of your days and life.

## Interaction

List two ways you can honor your parents today. Show your appreciation by writing them a thank-you note, making them breakfast, showing them more respect in public. You decide.

## Prayer

*Dear Lord, thank you for your Word. My prayer today is that I would respect and love my parents as you use me in the building of your kingdom. I pray that my respect for my parents will reflect my bad-to-the-bone commitment to be about your business like Jesus. In Jesus' name I pray, Amen.*

## Memory Verse

"Not everyone who says to Me, 'Lord, Lord,' shall enter the kingdom of heaven, but he who does the will of My Father in heaven."

Matthew 7:21

# THURSDAY

## A Growing Business

### Read Luke 2:39–50

Having a teenage daughter brings back memories of my relationship with my older sister. She constantly had friends over to our house. They'd listen to music, put on makeup, and share the latest gossip. As a younger brother it was my duty to disrupt their day as much as possible. I'd find practically any reason to barge into my sister's room, or I'd walk by the door about twenty times per minute just to check out her friends. If that didn't work, I'd make up reasons why she had to go downstairs: I'd tell her that Mom or Dad wanted to speak with her, she needed to clean up her mess in the kitchen, or the phone was for her (even though it hadn't even rung). What can I say? I was a twelve-year-old with no life of my own.

My sister was no dummy, though. She had her own weapons of warfare. Besides screaming about my antics to our mother, her favorite line to me was "Mind your own business, dog breath." I remember thinking to myself, *What is my business?*

I've learned since then that my business should be God's business— doing His will and spreading the Gospel. The same goes for you, too.

When Jesus was twelve, He not only knew what His Father wanted Him to do, He was doing it.

*"Why did you seek Me? Did you not know that I must be about My Father's business?"*

—*Luke 2:49*

The Bible says that Jesus came to preach the Gospel to the lost. Read the following verses and ask yourself if you are about your Father's business.

*The blind see and the lame walk; the lepers are cleansed and the deaf hear; the dead are raised up and the poor have the gospel preached to them.*

—Matthew 11:5–6

*For the Son of Man has come to seek and to save that which was lost.*

—Luke 19:10

*"The Spirit of the Lord is upon Me, because He has anointed Me to preach the gospel to the poor; he has sent Me to heal the brokenhearted, to proclaim liberty to the captives and recovery of sight to the blind, to set at liberty those who are oppressed."*

—Luke 4:18

Make a decision today to rebel against the business of trying to be popular or rich. Your business is to build riches in heaven. Your business is to share the Gospel, starting right now. You have what it takes, so begin investing today in your Father's Gospel-sharing business.

## Interaction

Write two things you can do today that involve your Father's business. Each day, try to increase the number of things you do for God until you find your life consumed with His business.

## Prayer

*Dear Lord, thank you for your Word. My prayer today is that I would be about your business. I pray that when my friends are worrying about dating and being popular, I will be most concerned about doing your will. I pray that my bad-to-the-bone preoccupation with my Father's business would truly reflect the godliness of Jesus. In Jesus' name I pray, Amen.*

## Memory Verse

"Not everyone who says to Me, 'Lord, Lord,' shall enter the kingdom of heaven, but he who does the will of My Father in heaven."

Matthew 7:21

# FRIDAY

# Let Me Ask You a Question
### Read Luke 2:39–50

When I fly to other cities for speaking engagements, someone from the sponsoring church or conference usually meets me at the airport. Last year at the Miami Airport I was picked up by a youth pastor and one of his teenage disciples, a sixteen-year-old football player with a huge interest in evangelism. During our one-hour drive to the conference center the teenager asked me about ninety-two questions regarding ministry. Anybody who knows me knows that I gave him an earful of answers.

When Jesus was in the temple, what was He doing? Asking questions.

*Now so it was that after three days they found Him in the temple, sitting in the midst of the teachers, both listening to them and asking them questions.*

*—Luke 2:46*

Asking questions is like talking through a two-way mirror. Sure, your questions get to the other side and information comes back to you. But your questions also reflect who you are. People learn about you from the types of questions you ask. The young football player's questions to me in Miami helped him find out about evangelism. But his many questions were also a clear sign to me that he was a sincere and committed Christian.

We see from the Bible that the rabbis were greatly impressed by the twelve-year-old boy who called himself Jesus.

*All who heard Him were astonished at His great understanding and answers.*

*—verse 47*

There's no mistaking that Jesus' answers impressed the rabbis. However, it's just as clear that His questions reflected His understanding of the Scriptures and other issues of faith. And sure enough, we learn in verse 52 that "Jesus increased in wisdom and stature, and in favor with God and men."

Jesus asked lots of questions throughout His life, and you should do the same. Get in the habit of asking questions when you want to learn something, especially from adults who you respect. It's easy to start, just begin with, "Hey, let me ask you a question, please . . ."

## Interaction

Find one, two, or three people in your church who are older and wiser than you, and commit to asking them questions when they come up.

## Prayer

*Dear Lord, thank you for your Word. My prayer today is that I would always seek your wisdom and knowledge. I know the Bible is your answer book, but I also know that you have placed in my life people who can provide me with information and guidance. I want to continue to grow in my knowledge of you so that one day I will be a bad-to-the-bone handler of your business, just like Jesus. In Jesus' name I pray, Amen.*

## Memory Verse

"Not everyone who says to Me, 'Lord, Lord,' shall enter the kingdom of heaven, but he who does the will of My Father in heaven."
Matthew 7:21

# WEEKEND WARRIOR
## Jesus
### Read Luke 2:46–47

Don't you wonder what the temple rabbis first thought when a twelve-year-old kid named Jesus invaded their turf? I can imagine someone saying, "What's up with this punk? Isn't He *ever* going to go home?"

Jesus had His own agenda, however. He planted himself in the temple because what He had to say and ask was of utmost importance. He wanted to have a serious discussion about God with the Bible teachers, and in no time, He and the rabbis started to dialogue.

> *After three days they found [Jesus] in the temple, sitting in the midst of the teachers, both listening to them and asking them questions. And all who heard Him were astonished at His understanding and answers.*
>
> —*Luke 2:46–47*

In today's world, it's incredibly important to talk about godly things with fellow Christians, to study the Bible together and learn what God is saying to us. We need to support each other. If necessary, we need to challenge each other.

Think about all the people who drive past churches without stopping in. It's clear that they're missing out on God. But is it any less sad that many people attend church but never take the time for a Bible class? How about the ones who overlook opportunities to simply sit down and discuss biblical matters with other believers?

When was the last time you spent time discussing eternal things with older and wiser believers? If your answer is *never* or *a long time ago*, it's about time you began to take seriously your need for Bible instruction.

You need to find someone who will sit with you and discuss the things of God. Decide what lessons from the Bible you need to learn, then make a commitment to improve your understanding and knowledge of God's Word.

## Interaction

Decide on a person or two at church with whom you can sit and ask three Bible-related questions. Meet them at church, and sit, talk, and learn.

## Prayer

*Dear Lord, thank you for your Word. I pray that today I will find a place that I can plant myself and learn about you from someone more educated than me. I pray that in church this weekend, you would send a bad-to-the-bone Christian who can help me better understand how your Word applies to my life so that I can be about your business like Jesus. In Jesus' name I pray, Amen.*

# WEEKEND WARRIOR

## Jesus

### Read Luke 2:25–38

Everything about Jesus' life on earth should be an example to us. The Bible says that He prayed often—sometimes all night in the mountains, other times early in the morning. He used God's Word in countless situations, such as the time He resisted the Devil's temptations in the desert. Everywhere He went, Jesus loved the unlovable, healed the unhealable, touched the untouchable, and forgave the unforgivable.

How people interacted with Jesus can also guide us in being more like Jesus. He did not need others to pray for Him or verify His calling, but that's exactly what happened when Jesus was very young. When Mary and Joseph brought Jesus to Jerusalem to be circumcised, Simeon praised God for sending His Son to save the world.

> *"Lord, now You are letting Your servant depart in peace, according to Your word; for my eyes have seen Your salvation which You have prepared before the face of all peoples, a light to bring revelation to the Gentiles, and the glory of Your people Israel."*
> —*Luke 2:29–32*

Moments later, a very old prophetess named Anna also recognized Jesus' holiness.

> *Coming in that instant she gave thanks to the Lord, and spoke of Him to all those who looked for redemption in Jerusalem.*
> —*verse 38*

Just as there were people who predicted and prayed for Jesus' ministry, so there are people who can pray for yours. Someone in your life has probably seen God's hand on you. Someone can help you identify God's calling for your life. I encourage you this weekend to seek people who can help you identify your God-given talents and calling.

## Interaction

Find someone (your pastor or youth pastor?) who can pray over your life and identify your gifts and God's calling.

## Prayer

*Dear Lord, thank you for your Word. I pray that today I can begin a successful project of finding someone who can help me identify the gifts you have given me. I want to live my life doing what you made me to do. I want those who are close to me to pray that I would do your will. I want to be about your business all the days of my life, just like Jesus. In Jesus' name I pray, Amen.*

# WEEK 6

## Be On Fire for the Lord Like Josiah

Josiah became king of Israel when he was only eight years old. Rather than being a third-grader, he was groomed as the spiritual and political leader of a nation. Millions of people depended on Josiah for leadership, and he provided it for thirty-one years.

One of Josiah's most important decisions, however, came at the age of sixteen; he decided that he did not need anyone to take him to church—he would go on his own. 2 Chronicles 34:3 says that Josiah sought the God of his fathers. He became on fire for the Lord.

This week the Holy Spirit will challenge you to be bad to the bone and on fire like Josiah. May God bless you as you study His Word.

# Memory Verse
# of the Week

"But seek first the kingdom of God and
His righteousness, and all these things shall
be added to you."

MATTHEW 6:33

# MONDAY

## This Faith Is Mine

### Read 2 Chronicles 34

As a youth pastor, I stressed the evangelical element of Sunday morning services. I was always preaching for salvation and challenging young people to bring their nonbelieving friends to church. We used music, skits, videos—all sorts of things—to present the Gospel.

Unfortunately, there'd be times when a few kids—usually sitting in the back row—would start talking and messing around during the message or altar call. I'd either signal a leader to quiet them down or I'd do it myself with a quick word from the pulpit. Every now and then, a kid or two would be so determined to make life miserable for everyone else that I'd have to kick them out and tell their parents not to bring them back until they could pay attention. It broke my heart knowing that these kids were cheating themselves out of the joy of walking with God, but I had to consider what was best for the church.

What are you like at church? Do your parents force you to go to church, or do you go without any prompting because you want to be there? Do you pray and read the Bible without being told? Do you seek God on your own?

When Josiah was sixteen, the Bible says that he sought God on his own. Basically, Josiah told his parents and friends, "I can't hang out today. I gotta go to church."

Are you lukewarm about Jesus? Can you take Him or leave Him? Let me tell you, don't be like the many kids (and adults) who do not begin to truly seek God until a crisis hits their life. Without Jesus, you will be miserable. Loser friends and the party scene will only destroy you. On the other hand, you can decide now to follow Jesus. You can decide to be on fire for Him. How? Start obeying everything you believe is His will for your life.

If you are already on fire for Jesus, keep the flames burning by staying faithful to the important things God calls us to do like reading the Bible, witnessing, and faithfully attending church.

Make a decision today to be on fire like Josiah.

## Interaction

Are you running from God? What do you think you will accomplish without God in your life?

## Prayer

*Dear Lord, thank you for your Word. I pray that you would open my eyes to my selfishness. Ignite a flame in my heart that will overcome any urge to complain about going to church. I pray that I will hunger and thirst for righteousness and godliness in my life. Fill my heart and mind with your desires so that I may live according to your Word and be on fire like Josiah. I want to be bad to the bone. In Jesus' name I pray, Amen.*

## Memory Verse

"But seek first the kingdom of God and His righteousness, and all these things shall be added to you."

Matthew 6:33

# TUESDAY

## Get In the Game

### Read 2 Chronicles 35

As you can tell, I don't hold back my opinions. When I was a new youth pastor, I had many ideas about how the church should be run. I wanted to have a youth-led worship band, videos related to the sermons, tons of greeters, etc. I wanted every teenager involved in some aspect of ministry. The problem was, there weren't enough adult leaders to help out.

Then one day, God spoke to me. *Use the teenagers themselves*, He said. And with that, God immediately began to call young people into leadership. They began doing all the things God had spoken to me about. As a matter of fact, so many young people got involved that it became the thing to do—almost a competition. Young people were practically standing in line to become leaders. They began to realize that they could be used by God. They started to seek God's power and might. They desired His grace and direction in their lives.

Josiah was that kind of a teenager. The Bible says that he reigned as king for thirty-one years, but he started early—at the age of eight.

It is never too early to get involved in God's work. It is never too early to begin allowing Him to use you for great and mighty things. How long will you wait before allowing God to use you to build His kingdom? God wants you to be on fire for Him right now.

### Interaction

There are many ways to get more involved in your church and youth group. For instance, you could help out with worship skits, play or sing with the worship team, be trained to disciple a younger person, join a prayer team, help with cleanup, greet newcomers, make announcements, even preach sermons. Pick one or two ideas from this list or your own and pray for an opportunity to serve.

## Prayer

*Dear Lord, thank you for your Word. I pray today that I can be used in the ministry. Help me identify my gifts and calling. Send a bad-to-the-bone believer into my life to help me see and understand the gifts you have given me. I pray that the Holy Spirit will show me what He wants me to do. I pray that I will be on fire like Josiah. In Jesus' name I pray, Amen.*

## Memory Verse

"But seek first the kingdom of God and His righteousness, and all these things shall be added to you."

Matthew 6:33

# WEDNESDAY

## Someone to Talk To

### Read 2 Chronicles 34:14–33

t never fails, after every service in every church several people will approach the pastor for counseling or an encouraging word. As you can imagine, people want to discuss anything and everything: personal salvation, problems with friends and family members, addictions, and so on. Pastors do have special insights, but mainly, people just need to talk to a caring and wise person about their current situation.

I try to help the best I can, but because I'm not always available to provide counsel, I often ask people if they have someone to talk to during the week.

Even Josiah, a great king with incredible responsibilities, needed counsel from people whom he trusted. When Hilkiah the high priest found the Book of the Covenant (probably an early version of the Book of Deuteronomy), Josiah told his advisors, "Go, inquire of the Lord for me, and for those who are left in Israel and Judah, concerning the words of the book that is found" (2 Chronicles 34:21). The people of Jerusalem had not kept the Lord's commands according to the Book of the Law, and Josiah knew that he needed help and support.

Do you have someone you can talk to when you need guidance? In Week Ten of this devotional, we discuss the need for a mentor or discipler, but the Bible says that we should really have several people to talk to about various concerns.

*Where there is no counsel, the people fall; but in the multitude of counselors there is safety.*

*—Proverbs 11:14*

Begin praying that God would send wise people into your life with whom you can talk about concerns.

## Interaction

List five areas of your life for which you'd like encouragement and wisdom (school issues, career choices, questions about dating, ministry options, spiritual gifts, Bible questions, etc.). Try to think of ten bad-to-the-bone people you can go to with concerns (parents, neighbors, pastors, church leaders, boss or supervisor at work, teachers, relatives, coaches, etc.). Match each of the five areas of concern with two names from your list.

## Prayer

*Dear Lord, thank you for your Word. I pray that I would find a group of people that will give me wisdom and encouragement when I need it. I know that in order to stay on fire for you, I must stay encouraged and resist trying to fight Satan alone. Please, God, show me where I most need wisdom and counsel and give me the courage to ask a multitude of bad-to-the-bone counselors for help. In Jesus' name I pray, Amen.*

## Memory Verse

"But seek first the kingdom of God and His righteousness, and all these things shall be added to you."

Matthew 6:33

# THURSDAY

## Fire Me Up

### Read 2 Chronicles 34:1–7; 35:29–33

Have you heard the saying, "You can lead a horse to water but you can't make him drink"? Well, don't believe it. It's all a matter of making that imaginary horse thirsty enough. For instance, even though I would never do this, what would happen if I took the horse for a long, long run on a hot day, maybe put some salt in his mouth, then brought him to some water? I'm pretty sure that he'd be ready to drain a small lake.

This same principle applies to spiritual matters. People who are truly thirsty for spiritual meaning, purpose, and security in life seek God more diligently than others. They find themselves on fire for God. I'm talking about people who seek God from morning to night and look forward to praying and learning about spiritual issues. Unfortunately, far too few people are on fire for God.

From where I stand, the number one reason people lack that fire is because they don't see the need to be on fire. They don't realize the intensity of our spiritual battles with the Devil and how much we need God.

Josiah had the big-time responsibility of running a nation and knew he needed God. He also knew that the entire country needed God. Years of worshiping false idols had left Israel spiritually dead. When Josiah thought about all that had to be done, he probably felt helpless. But when he included God in the picture, he got fired up. He had false idols and their altars destroyed. He called everyone together to hear God's covenant and observe Passover in the reconsecrated temple. And then he later went off to fight wars and defend the country.

Not sure how much you need God? Think about what life would be like without God. What kinds of things would be impossible for you to do? What responsibilities could you never fulfill?

## Interaction

Throughout 2 Chronicles 34 and 35, we see the spiritual reforms ordered by Josiah. List the spiritual reforms that you need God to bring about in your life. What changes in attitude and behavior are necessary?

## Prayer

*Dear Lord, thank you for your Word. I pray that you would fulfill Psalm 139:23–24 in my life: "Search me, O God, and know my heart; try me, and know my anxieties; and see if there is any wicked way in me, and lead me in the way everlasting." Lord, I surrender my heart to you, so that I would do whatever you want. Please ignite a bad-to-the-bone flame in me so that I may be on fire like Josiah. In Jesus' name I pray, Amen.*

## Memory Verse

"But seek first the kingdom of God and His righteousness, and all these things shall be added to you."

Matthew 6:33

# FRIDAY

## Faith: Fuel to the Fire

### Read 2 Chronicles 33:21–25; 34:1–2

One Saturday my family and I rented a small motorboat on a nearby lake. Of course, all three kids wanted to be captain. It was a bit tricky, though. To turn left, you needed to push the motor's handle to the right, and vice versa. My oldest daughter and my son got the hang of it rather quickly, but my middle daughter had a tough time. She found herself turning the opposite way she wanted to go, and kept steering us into the weeds. Frustration turned into wanting to give up. She just didn't want to mess up anymore.

Lots of people fear failing so much that they give up or they don't even try something challenging in the first place. Well, I wasn't going to let my daughter quit. I knew she could learn to steer the boat. And with a little more instruction and encouragement, she was buzzing around the lake in no time. All I had to do was point where I wanted to go and she'd take us there. She felt so good about herself that she didn't want to give up her spot in the captain's chair.

My kids didn't understand how the motor worked or why the boat floated. All they knew was that when you held on to the handle and turned the throttle, the boat went. In the spiritual sense, we need to learn the same lesson. When we hold on to God and turn on our faith, good things happen.

Josiah was a teenager who lived by faith as he ruled an entire country. He quickly learned to rest solely on God's faithfulness. Josiah didn't listen to the latest gossip or follow the coolest fads.

*He did what was right in the sight of the Lord, and walked in the*

103

*ways of his father David; he did not turn aside to the right hand or to the left.*

—2 Chronicles 34:2

Josiah chose to follow God. He believed that God's Word was the guideline by which to live, and he made the necessary changes in Israel to make things right.

## Interaction

In what area of your life has God been challenging you to take a step of faith? Write it down and make a commitment to do something by faith in that area today.

## Prayer

*Dear Lord, thank you for your Word. I pray that today I can take steps of faith, concentrating only on your will so that I never veer left or right. I want to live by faith, not by sight or fear. I want to see miracles happen in and around my life. Please give me bad-to-the-bone faith to be on fire like Josiah. In Jesus' name I pray, Amen.*

## Memory Verse

"But seek first the kingdom of God and His righteousness, and all these things shall be added to you."

Matthew 6:33

# WEEKEND WARRIOR

## Jairus's Daughter
### Read Mark 5:21–24, 35–43

t breaks my heart to hear young people talk about being in no-win situations. They have problems stacked on problems stacked on more problems. I want to help, but sometimes I don't know what to say or where to start. That's where Jesus comes in. He is the miracle worker. And if we believe in our Lord, we'll find that no problem is too big for Him.

Are you or a friend facing a hopeless situation? Does it involve thoughts of suicide? Worries about a possible pregnancy? Struggles with drugs? The prospect of jail time? Perhaps there's the added feeling of being abandoned at this crucial time? Whatever the situation, Jesus has already proven that He cares. Just look at what He did for Jairus's daughter.

*And behold, one of the rulers of the synagogue came, Jairus by name. And when he saw [Jesus], he fell at His feet and begged Him earnestly, saying, "My little daughter lies at the point of death. Come and lay Your hands on her, that she may be healed, and she will live." So Jesus went with him, and a great multitude followed Him and thronged Him.*

—Mark 5:22–24

While on their way to Jairus's house, however, some people rushed forward saying, "Your daughter is dead. Why trouble the Teacher any further?" (verse 35).

Does that sound like something Satan would say? He wants us to lose hope. He will even try to convince us that we shouldn't bother Jesus when we need help. But one of the best things about the Lord is that He is the source of all hope. And Jesus did not want Jairus to lose hope for one second. Verse 36 tells us, "As soon as Jesus heard the word that was spoken, He said to the ruler of the synagogue, 'Do not be afraid; only believe.' " This is the million-dollar word of encouragement from the Lord today: Do not be afraid; only believe.

Today you must decide to believe that Jesus is not only able to help you but willing. The size of the miracle you are willing to allow to happen will be directly related to your belief in the power of the God you are praying to for that miracle. Therefore, the question you must ask yourself is, How big is my God? Did your God really create the heavens and the earth? Did your God really create the plants, fish, birds, and people? If your God did all of that, why can't He perform the miracle you're praying for?

## Interaction

List all the impossible situations facing you or someone you love. Review that list. I challenge you to find even one thing that God cannot resolve. Nothing is impossible with God. If He can raise a little girl from the dead, He can certainly help you quit taking drugs or find a godly boyfriend or girlfriend or improve your grades or help you be obedient to His commands.

## Prayer

*Dear Lord, thank you for your Word. I pray that I will trust you no matter what I am facing. I pray that even if everyone has lost hope, I will believe. I will trust you. I will have faith. You know the impossible situations I face, so I pray that you would take over. Jesus said in Matthew 11:28–30: "Come to Me, all you who labor and are heavy laden, and I will give you rest. Take My yoke upon you and learn from Me, for I am gentle and lowly in heart, and you will find rest for your souls. For My yoke is easy and My burden is light." Lord, I come to you and I cast my heavy burdens on you, trusting that you will give me rest. In Jesus' name I pray, Amen.*

# WEEKEND WARRIOR

## Jairus's Daughter

### Read Mark 5:21–24, 35–43

I n this weekend's Scripture reading, did you notice the interesting thing Jesus did once Jairus's daughter was raised from the dead? Before I get to that, however, let me reset the scene.

Remember, the twelve-year-old girl was dead—people were mourning—but Jesus walked up to her and saw an opportunity to glorify His Father. He boldly announced, "Why make this commotion and weep? The child is not dead, but sleeping" (Mark 5:39). The crowd's response? They laughed at Him.

> Then [Jesus] took the child by the hand, and said to her, "Talitha, cumi," which is translated, "Little girl, I say to you, arise." Immediately the girl arose and walked, for she was twelve years of age. And they were overcome with great amazement.
> —verses 41–42

Now, what happened next is what I find so interesting, so amazing: After raising Jairus's daughter from the dead, Jesus told the crowd that "something should be given her to eat" (verse 43). Isn't that incredible? Jesus is sensitive to our *every* need. He is concerned about the big and small issues in life—from drug addictions and gang involvement to math tests and sporting events.

Jesus said you should cast *all* your cares on Him, not just the big ones. He loves you so much that He died for *all* your sins, not just the ones that you cannot handle. Get into the habit of telling Jesus about everything in your life. The Bible says we are to pray without ceasing (1 Thessalonians 5:17). That means all-day, nonstop conversation with God. He wants to consume your life and handle every situation you face.

## Interaction

List five things that you don't regularly pray about because you think they are too small or simple to bother God with. Make a commitment to hand them over to the Lord each day.

## Prayer

*Dear Lord, thank you for your Word, and thank you for being sensitive to my every need. I pray that I will never think anything is too small for you to handle. I pray that I will get in the habit of coming to you with all of my problems, knowing that you want to relieve my light and heavy burdens. In Jesus' name I pray, Amen.*

# WEEK 7

## Be Holy Like Mary

She was a young teen, engaged to be married. Her future husband was a godly and well-respected man in the community. Mary had her entire future ahead—everything seemed to going according to schedule—and then BAM, she was pregnant. But how? She had never had sex.

Think about how Mary must have felt, dealing with the pressures. (In those days, the penalty for being pregnant and unmarried was death.) Can you imagine Mary wondering why she had been picked to be the mother of Jesus Christ? How would she raise the Son of God?

One thing's certain, Mary's holiness kept her strong and totally set aside for God's purpose. This week the Holy Spirit will challenge you to be bad-to-the-bone holy like Mary. May God bless you as you study His Word.

# Memory Verse
# of the Week

"Be holy, for I am holy."

1 PETER 1:16

# MONDAY
## Fruit of the Womb
### Read Luke 1

If you ever want to witness the dangers of drug use, visit a hospital that treats babies who are born addicted to drugs. Undersized infants with their ribs showing shake in their cribs. There are needles in their arms, tubes in their noses, and wires taped to their tiny bodies monitoring vital signs. All this because their mothers filled their bodies with unhealthy chemicals. As a result, the fruit or product of their womb was not healthy.

When I think of the holiness of Mary, it went beyond spiritual purity. She was also pure in body and mind. As her cousin Elizabeth said, "Blessed are you among women, and blessed is the fruit of your womb!" (Luke 1:42). Mary was a physical vessel through which the Son of God came. Her body was used to nourish the physical body of the baby Jesus.

You, too, must live a life that produces godly offspring. Malachi 2:15 says the Lord "seeks godly offspring," so by faith you must flee sexual immorality. By faith you must honor your body as the temple of the Holy Spirit by staying away from drugs, alcohol, and cigarettes. By faith you must keep God first by being faithful in prayer, Bible study, and fellowship with believers.

Having godly offspring may be the furthest thing from your mind, but if and when you do have children, you will be responsible for their health and development. The purity of your life will definitely affect the fruit of your life—spiritually, emotionally, mentally, and physically. This applies to men just as much as women. The Bible says that the man is the priest of the home. It is the dad's responsibility to lead the family in living for the Lord. He does this through his godly example.

Now is a great time to pray for the fruit of your life. Pray that you will be a qualified vessel of God to bring into this world a baby who would bless the world; a baby who is not only physically healthy but emotionally, mentally, and spiritually willing and able to honor God in all things.

## Interaction

List three ways to ensure that the fruit of your body will be blessed.

## Prayer

*Dear Lord, thank you for your Word. I pray that I would be a pure vessel for your good. I want the fruit of my body to be blessed, healthy, and productive. I want to produce a godly offspring. I pray that the fruit of my life will be useful in your kingdom. May I be bad-to-the-bone holy like Mary. In Jesus' name I pray, Amen.*

## Memory Verse

"Be holy, for I am holy."

1 Peter 1:16

# TUESDAY

## Holy

### Read Luke 1:26–30

When my wife was pregnant with our first child I was convinced that we would have a girl. And sure enough, we were blessed with the little girl I had always wanted. Being a new dad and all, I was extremely protective. I did not want people kissing her, holding her, or spending too much time with her. One day I broke down and let someone hold her while I ate dinner. Well, my daughter fell asleep near the woman's neck, and when I got her back she smelled like perfume for a week. You better believe that was the last time I let her fall asleep on someone. I wanted her all to myself. I did not want the influence of the world on her. She was just a baby, but I had already determined that there was no way I'd let her use drugs, smoke, use bad language, or become sexually active before marriage. I wanted her to be holy; set aside for one purpose—God's purpose.

God wants you and me to be holy; set aside just for Him. The Bible says that God loves us with a jealous love. His love is so much better than anything we can find that He wants us to enjoy only it.

Mary was holy. She was set aside entirely for God's use. She did not split her affections between God and desires of the world. To ungodly things, Mary said, "Back off." Her only desire was to serve and please her heavenly Father. In today's Scripture reading, notice how Mary is described:

- 𝄞 "virgin"—No man had ever touched her.
- 𝄞 "highly favored"—God had chosen her for a specific duty.
- 𝄞 "blessed among women"—She was content and people spoke well of her.

Are you holy? Are you set aside just for God? Or is He sharing you with something else? Money? Athletics? A boyfriend or girlfriend? A car? It's not a sin to have any of these, but they should never ever take the place of God in your heart. Remember, no one or no thing will ever love you more completely and faithfully than the Lord. Make a decision today to surrender your entire life to Him.

## Interaction

List three things in your life God has to share you with.

## Prayer

*Dear Lord, thank you for your Word. I pray that I would be set apart for your purposes. I don't want anything to come between us, Lord. Please take away my desire for things that come between us, and give me the desire to be close to you. May this closeness make me bad-to-the-bone holy like Mary. In Jesus' name I pray, Amen.*

## Memory Verse

"Be holy, for I am holy."

1 Peter 1:16

# WEDNESDAY
## Humble Pie
### Luke 1:26–38

Tell me if this sounds familiar. It's election time at school for student body government. Around the school hang posters from the candidates—all saying that they're the best person for the job because of this reason or that. Election day comes, and when the winners are announced they rejoice and even strut. They're "da bomb," and they know it.

God's looking for good people, too, but He has no need for people who strut. He's looking for preachers, teachers, and prayer warriors whose humble prayers will oppose spiritual forces of darkness. He's looking for people who will serve the poor and needy; people who will take the Gospel to those who have never heard it before. In order to be used by God, you don't need a lot of experience, education, money, or popularity with man, but you do need humility. God wants people who realize that He is the one who makes their accomplishments possible.

Imagine being hand-picked by God to become the parent of His one and only Son. Quite an honor, huh? But did Mary get a big head? Did she strut around knowing the angel told her that God had personally picked her as the best earthly-mother-of-God candidate? Of course not. Mary expressed surprise and humbly accepted the responsibility.

*Mary said to the angel, "How can this be, since I do not know a man?" . . . Then Mary said, "Behold the maidservant of the Lord! Let it be to me according to your word." And the angel departed from her.*

—Luke 1:34, 38

Mary knew that she was low, in comparison to God. Her mind was focused so much on God's promises and faithfulness that she did not have time to praise herself. Without God, Mary was a sinner, hopeless and helpless. But with God, she was bad-to-the-bone holy.

## Interaction

List three things that have happened in the past week or two that only God could have done.

## Prayer

*Dear Lord, thank you for your Word. My prayer today is that I will always remember that my achievements are possible only through you. Keep me humble and let praise always be on my lips, no matter the circumstances. May I always acknowledge your goodness to me. Please help me to be holy like Mary. In Jesus' name I pray, Amen.*

## Memory Verse

"Be holy, for I am holy."

1 Peter 1:16

# THURSDAY

## Have It Your Way, God!

### Read Luke 1

When my brother played college football in upstate New York, I was able to attend only one game. They were playing Colgate University. Don threw four touchdown passes in the first half, and they won easily.

After the game we were walking down the street when a young woman approached us. As she neared, her eyes got big and she began to smile.

"Are you Don McPherson?"

"Yes," my brother said.

And with that, she grabbed his hand and kissed it.

*This is ridiculous*, I thought to myself. Apparently my brother enjoyed the attention—or maybe he was in shock like me—because he sure didn't do anything to stop her.

When good things happen to you, I'm guessing that you don't object. But how do you react when bad things happen?

When Mary found herself pregnant with no husband, in a culture where she could have been killed for such a thing, what was her attitude? She remained faithful to God and ignored the certain questions and gossip. Her actions spoke: You can think what you want, but I am sticking with God.

Will you be so quick to accept the good with the bad like Mary? This, too, is part of being holy, and absolutely necessary for all bad-to-the-bone believers.

### Interaction

Do you remember how you responded the last time something bad happened to you? Write down a summary, then write what you should have said or done. Make a commitment to respond like Mary the next time you face an unpleasant situation.

## Prayer

*Dear Lord, thank you for your Word. I pray that I would accept, unconditionally, whatever you ask me to go through today. I realize that you did not complain when you died on the cross for me. The least I can do is accept, learn, and grow from whatever you want me to go through. I pray that you will use my life according to your will. I pray that I will be holy like Mary. In Jesus' name I pray, Amen.*

## Memory Verse

"Be holy, for I am holy."

1 Peter 1:16

# FRIDAY

## Good Is Good Enough

### Read Luke 1

While preparing for a youth crusade in Texas, I spent an entire week conducting high school assemblies. I talked about abstinence, drug abuse, gang involvement, and self-esteem to assemblies packed with five hundred to two thousand students each. I did my best to fill the presentations with laughter, but we also covered a lot of thought-provoking issues. I shared some of the horror stories of my younger days: how I used drugs, messed around with girls, and almost ruined my life by making the wrong choices. Back then I was no different than the many other young people who live in the fast lane, trying to find happiness in all the wrong places.

Some friends of mine from San Diego had come along to help with the crusade. One of them was Jimmy, a faithful young man who had never done drugs or alcohol. He had never had sex or even said a curse word. He was one of those rare kids who stayed away from all of those sinful ways.

Driving back to the hotel one day, Jimmy mentioned that he wished he hadn't been such a "good" kid. He thought his testimony would be more effective if he had experienced the things of the world.

This is simply not true. It is how God can use you for good that makes your life a powerful testimony, not how much evil you have done. God is looking for people who are holy and unspotted from the world—people who have been set aside for His purpose; people who have been faithful over a long period. Mary was such a person. From her childhood, she was kept aside just for God's use, and in return, God chose her to bring His Son into the world.

No matter what your history, good or bad, if you ask God to forgive your sins, repent, and commit your life to Him, He will use you to build His kingdom. Good is good enough, and being holy is the most effective testimony around.

## Interaction

List three positive things about your life to build upon and make even stronger. Write down one strategy for each that will help in that development.

## Prayer

*Dear Lord, thank you for your Word. I pray that I will appreciate the good in my life, knowing that all good things are from you. Thank you for protecting me from sin. I will always work at becoming a better person, but I know that being good is good enough for you. Let me be a godly, bad-to-the-bone example to those around me, Lord. Set me aside so that I am holy like Mary. In Jesus' name I pray, Amen.*

## Memory Verse

"Be holy, for I am holy."

1 Peter 1:16

# WEEKEND WARRIOR
## Herodias' Daughter
### Read Mark 6:14–29

One evening a young man and his stepdaughter stopped me after a church service. He explained to me that the seventeen-year-old girl was dancing illegally as a stripper in a local nightclub. She had moved out of the house and was living with another stripper.

As we talked, I shared with her verses from the Bible concerning lust and the appearance of evil. She began to cry but remained defiant about continuing to dance. I tried a different approach.

"How would you feel if someone you knew, someone you respected, came and watched you dance?"

"Embarrassed."

"But why, if there's nothing wrong with it?"

The Bible says that the heart knows its own bitterness (Proverbs 14:10). There is no way you can justify sin. God is watching you. Whether you are a girl or a guy, God has given you the ability to charm and to be sweet; you must not allow the Devil to use this for evil. Not only will you hurt others, you will hurt yourself.

In today's Bible reading, Herodias' daughter made two very bad mistakes. First, she danced for Herod and the other men in his government.

*And when Herodias' daughter herself came in and danced, and pleased Herod and those who sat with him, the king said to the girl, "Ask me whatever you want, and I will give it to you." He also swore to her, "Whatever you ask me, I will give you, up to half of my kingdom."*

*—Mark 6:22–23*

The girl's second mistake occurred when she sought advice from her mother, an evil woman; in fact, the woman with whom Herod was committing adultery. The daughter's request? The head of John the Baptist.

Herodias' daughter used her beauty to have John the Baptist killed. How are you using your beauty? (Guys need to consider this question, too. They can also use their good looks in sinful ways.) Are you using your body for God's glory or your own? Are you using it to take advantage of people, sharing it with whoever wants pleasure, or are you saving it for your future spouse?

This weekend make a fresh commitment not to misuse your beauty or charm. It is God-given, so let God use it.

## Interaction

Make a commitment in writing not to use your beauty or charm to sin, do evil, or cause someone else to sin. Tell someone you trust about this commitment and ask them to help you stay pure.

## Prayer

*Dear Lord, thank you for your Word. I pray that starting this weekend I will not use my beauty for selfish gain. I pray that I can allow you to be glorified in everything I do. I want to surrender my whole self into your hands. In Jesus' name I pray, Amen.*

# WEEKEND WARRIOR
## Herodias' Daughter
### Read Matthew 14:1–12

learned at a very young age to respect my elders; not only my relatives but all adults. Talking back to an adult was not an option. I just accepted that because they were older, they knew better. But the older I got, the more I realized that this was not necessarily so. As I grew as a Christian I further realized that some adults are ungodly. Their advice should not be trusted; the way they live should not be an example.

In this weekend's Bible reading, Herodias twice failed in her duty as a mother. First, she should not have let her daughter dance for the men. Second, she should not have encouraged her to ask to kill someone. We don't know if the daughter questioned this advice, but the result was anything but good.

Satan—through other people or through the lust of your flesh—will try to use your beauty to "ask for someone's head on a platter." He might tempt you to use your popularity to make someone dislike another person. He might tempt you to use your smile and pretty face to entice someone into an immoral relationship.

> For by means of a harlot a man is reduced to a crust of bread; and an adulteress will prey upon his precious life.
> —Proverbs 6:26

Herodias' daughter did not have the maturity to do the right things. She did not have the maturity to acknowledge that her mom was wrong. She totally ignored Psalm 1:1 which says, "Blessed is the man who walks not in the counsel of the ungodly."

Always keep in mind that you alone will pay for your actions. Decisions should be based on what you believe will honor God. This is why it is so important to know God's counsel and wisdom.

## Interaction

Are you paying the consequences for a decision you made based on someone else's bad advice? Write about the situation and the decision you *should* have made.

## Prayer

*Dear Lord, thank you for your Word. I pray that I would learn to trust your Word more than any person. I know that there will be times in my life when someone will give me bad advice. Please help me to know the difference between what you want and what others want. In Jesus' name I pray, Amen.*

# WEEK 8

## Be a Virgin Like Rebekah

Rebekah was a young woman who would eventually become one of the most significant mothers in the Bible. You might know her son by the name *Israel*. Before Rebekah married Isaac, however, Genesis 24:16 says, "The young woman was very beautiful to behold, a virgin; no man had known her."

In today's society, virgins are rarer than ever. Still, virginity is and will always be God's standard for single people. If you have sinned sexually, this is the perfect time to ask God for forgiveness and to repent. 1 John 1:9 says, "If we confess our sins, He is faithful and just to forgive us our sins and to cleanse us from all unrighteousness."

If you have committed sexual sin, take a moment to pray that God would forgive you and restore your spiritual virginity. Ask Him to give you the desire and strength to remain pure until the day you are married. Remember, God is a God of second chances.

This week the Holy Spirit will challenge you to live the bad-to-the-bone life of a virgin like Rebekah. May God bless you as you study His Word.

# Memory Verse
# of the Week

Flee sexual immorality. Every sin that a man
does is outside the body, but he who
commits sexual immorality sins against his
own body.

1 CORINTHIANS 6:18

# MONDAY

## No Virtual Virgin Here

### Read Genesis 24

One day I was walking through the airport when I saw a young woman wearing a very short skirt. It was hilarious, because every two steps she would grab that mini-mini dress and try to stretch it longer. Everyone was looking, but she didn't seem to mind. As I passed her, I couldn't resist asking, "Why don't you just buy a longer skirt?" She rolled her eyes and walked on, tugging her skirt.

I understand why some people want to be noticed, to be the focus of attention. But if you do it by flaunting your stuff, do you realize the message you're sending? To be blunt, it gives the impression that you want some action.

This was definitely not the case with Rebekah. When Abraham's servant met Rebekah, the Bible says she was working hard and she was a virgin. ("Now the young woman was very beautiful to behold, a virgin; no man had known her" Genesis 24:16.) Even though it is not stated in this Bible passage, in those days, young women who were virgins often wore special robes to signify their virginity. For instance, 2 Samuel 13:18 says Tamar wore "a robe of many colors, for the king's virgin daughters wore such apparel." These young women were proud of their virginity. Their purity was a thing of honor.

Rebekah was a young woman with honor. She was proud that no man had ever touched her. She knew that she was not cheap. She had a high sense of value and respect for her body and sexuality.

Whether or not your friends and classmates think so, God wants and commands us to be sexually pure before marriage. Now, it's important to understand that sexual sin affects you beyond the physical aspect. It hurts you mentally, emotionally, and spiritually. Sexual sin affects your mental self by leaving unwanted memories, thoughts, and images in your mind. Your emotions get tossed around, and feelings often become too harsh to handle. Most importantly, though, sexual sin endangers your relationship with Christ.

> *The body is not for sexual immorality but for the Lord, and the Lord for the body. . . . Do you not know that your bodies are members of Christ? Shall I then take the members of Christ and make them members of a harlot? Certainly not!*
> —*1 Corinthians 6:13, 15*

Sexual purity protects you from harm. God desires your whole being to be pure and that you avoid any appearance of evil in how you conduct your life. There should be no inconsistencies about your life; nothing virtual about who you are and what you stand for. Ask yourself what message your appearance sends. Does it say that you are sexually pure or sexually active? What message do you send by the way you talk to members of the opposite sex or look at them? Whether you are a virgin or not, you can be sexually pure from this point forward, and that purity extends throughout your thoughts and actions. Purpose in your heart to be a pure virgin inside and out like Rebekah.

## Interaction

Some people have different ideas of what constitutes a sexual sin. What do you think being a virgin means? Talk about it with your parents or youth group leaders.

## Prayer

*Dear Lord, thank you for your Word. I realize that virginity means being pure both inside and out. I pray that I would be purified in my mind, heart, soul, and body. Make me aware of my hidden sins, and keep me away from all sin. I pray for a bad-to-the-bone thirst for holiness and sexual purity so that I can be a virgin like Rebekah. In Jesus' name I pray, Amen.*

## Memory Verse

Flee sexual immorality. Every sin that a man does is outside the body, but he who commits sexual immorality sins against his own body.

1 Corinthians 6:18

# TUESDAY

## Get Accountability

### Read Genesis 24:22–58

Let me give it to you straight: Sexual pressure is real, and the opportunity to sin sexually will come your way often, but the consequences are even more real and long lasting. If you sin sexually, you will pay for it more than any other sin. Here's why: Sexual sin is the only sin that is committed against the body. 1 Corinthians 6:18 says, "Flee sexual immorality. Every sin that a man does is outside the body, but he who commits sexual immorality sins against his own body."

God always holds us accountable. Therefore, it is very important to do everything in your power to avoid sexual sin. One of the first steps is to ask one or more responsible adults and friends to help in keeping yourself accountable. Parents, teachers, mentors, and youth leaders can all encourage and help you stay pure.

Several verses in Genesis 24 provide other good steps to follow to remain pure:

- Verses 24–28 show Rebekah's relationship with her family. She is not alone in her decision-making process, and she lets the messenger know that. It is important to be submissive to people over you who have more wisdom and experience than you do.
- Verse 51 shows us that Rebekah asked her family for permission to go with Abraham's servant. Before dating anyone, get permission from your parents; talk about it with your accountability group. In fact, they should even talk with the person you want to date to judge his or her worthiness. The Bible says that there is safety in the multitude of counsel. The more people involved in this process, the safer you will be.

✗ Verses 57–58 reveal that Rebekah's family, after providing their input, allowed her to make the final decision about going with the servant. Your accountability group must know you well enough to determine what decisions you should and should not make. You won't make the right decision each and every time—none of us do—but you will be responsible for the consequences of that decision.

## Interaction

List the names of people with whom you can have honest conversations about dating and sexual issues. Ask them to be your accountability partners.

## Prayer

*Dear Lord, thank you for your Word. Lord, please help me develop strong relationships with people who will be sensitive to my needs, weaknesses, and strengths when it comes to dating issues. I want to find people who will help me make responsible decisions. I pray that you would send a bad-to-the-bone believer who can help me be a virgin like Rebekah. In Jesus' name I pray, Amen.*

## Memory Verse

Flee sexual immorality. Every sin that a man does is outside the body, but he who commits sexual immorality sins against his own body.

1 Corinthians 6:18

# WEDNESDAY

## God Will Provide

### Read Genesis 24

Every week in church, just before the sermon, the pastor urges everyone to take a minute to say hello to someone they don't know. One Sunday, during this brief fellowship time, my friend Ann turned around and introduced herself to a guy named Dan. Well, after talking awhile, they not only exchanged names, they also traded phone numbers. Sometime later, they began to date. Today, Ann and Dan are happily married, living proof that when God wants you to date or marry a certain person, He will send that person into your life.

That's exactly what God did when Adam was lonely in the Garden of Eden. As earth's only human, Adam desperately wanted companionship, so God brought to him every animal. Adam gave them all names, but none was suitable as his helper or wife. Fortunately, Adam wasn't the only one who knew that four-legged beasts wouldn't cut it as companions. God knew it, too, and in nothing flat He created Eve.

God hasn't changed since then. He knows what we need and what we desire. He created physical desires, and He created marriage to satisfy those desires. If you wait for God's direction about dating and marriage, you will be blessed. If you try to force the issue by chasing someone based solely on their looks or some other feature rather than listening for God's wisdom, you will experience heartache and pain.

Rebekah wasn't looking for a man or trying to be cute when she met her future husband, Isaac. She had remained pure before marriage; maybe even used lines like "I said no, Joe" or "Stand back, Jack" or "Take a hike, Ike" to keep her purity intact. In reward, God gave Rebekah a bad-to-the-bone husband, Isaac. If God worked their relationship out, don't you think He'll do the same for you? If you believe this and trust God, He will help you remain pure as you wait patiently for that special person. For guys and girls, that's what it takes to be a virgin like Rebekah.

## Interaction

List the consequences of taking dating matters into your own hands.

## Prayer

*Dear Lord, thank you for your Word. I pray that I would have supernatural patience and trust to wait for your perfect mate at the perfect time. Please give me direction on how to use my time. I want to be a virgin like Rebekah. In Jesus' name I pray, Amen.*

## Memory Verse

Flee sexual immorality. Every sin that a man does is outside the body, but he who commits sexual immorality sins against his own body.

1 Corinthians 6:18

# THURSDAY

## Hardworking Woman

### Read Genesis 24:15–24

When I was young, it seemed like every movie showed a young lady spending the entire day making herself beautiful, waiting for the perfect guy to sweep her off her feet.

Get real. Obviously, life doesn't work that way, but every now and then I meet a highly misled young woman who believes that all she has to do is be beautiful and one day some guy will come along, marry her, and take care of all their needs. Similarly, I sometimes meet guys who think life is going to be a breeze; that a good job will just flow their way and they'll make lots of money with little effort.

Rebekah didn't fall for either of these traps. She was a hard worker and didn't sit around beautifying herself all day. Instead, she spent her day carrying water pots, watering camels, and serving others.

One of the keys to being sexually pure is to keep your mind off sexual things and instead focus on work: helping your parents around the house or in the yard, staying on top of your school work, being a good employee at your job. All of these "distractions" actually play an important role in your development as a responsible young adult. They build a strong, consistent character—one that will be well prepared to make tough decisions, especially in the area of relationships.

If you want to be sexually pure like Rebekah, be heavenly minded and decide in your heart that you are going to be a hard worker as it pertains to the things of God. Whatever God's calling—difficult or easy—you will be committed to doing it.

### Interaction

What work has God put before you? In what jobs or responsibilities do you need to become a hard worker?

## Prayer

*Dear Lord, thank you for your Word. I pray that I will be a hard worker, and I trust that this will build a strong character within me. By being disciplined and bad to the bone I pray that I will be better equipped to be holy and sexually pure just like Rebekah. In Jesus' name I pray, Amen.*

## Memory Verse

Flee sexual immorality. Every sin that a man does is outside the body, but he who commits sexual immorality sins against his own body.

1 Corinthians 6:18

# FRIDAY

## Love Me Right

### Read Genesis 24

've lost count of the teenage couples who have boldly told me that they were going to marry each other after graduating. They're in love, they say, their relationship perfect and never-ending. Some of these couples are only thirteen or fourteen years old at the time! Nice kids, but clueless. I'm all for people wanting positive things for themselves, but it's dangerous when you start making these sorts of commitments. For guys especially, all this love talk can lead to expecting sex. But that's not the definition of love.

Jesus tells us, "You shall love the Lord your God with all your heart, with all your soul, and with all your mind. This is the first and great commandment" (Matthew 22:37–38). And how should we show God that we love Him? Again, Jesus is the Answer Man: "If you love Me, keep My commandments" (John 14:15). Therefore, if someone says they love you, they should be committed to helping you obey God. If they ask you to do something that is against God's commandments, they don't love you, they lust you.

Many teenagers and young adults make long-term promises of marriage and faithfulness to each other, and then live as though the promises are already fulfilled. In other words, they think that because they intend to marry each other, they can act like they are married and have sex. Some even go so far as to live together. But the Bible clearly says that sex before marriage, or fornication, is a sin, and fornicators will not inherit the kingdom of God.

*Therefore be imitators of God as dear children. And walk in love, as Christ also has loved us and given Himself for us, an offering and a sacrifice to God for a sweet-smelling aroma. But fornication and all uncleanness or covetousness, let it not even be named among you, as is fitting for saints. . . . For this you know, that no fornicator, unclean person, nor covetous man, who is an idolater, has any inheritance in the kingdom of Christ and God.*

*—Ephesians 5:1–3, 5*

When you read the story of Rebekah, you read about a young, hard-working woman, a virgin, who was picked to marry a very powerful man. She accepted the invitation, and when she became Isaac's wife, he loved her.

Until you are married, with a ring on your finger and the marriage license in the drawer, you have no right to have sex with anyone. Solomon's Song of Songs says, "Do not stir up nor awaken love until it pleases" (3:5). There is a wrong time and a right time to have sex. The right time is after you are married. If it happens too soon, it's a sin that will hurt you and hurt God. To be sexually pure like Rebekah, be patient and wait until you're married.

## Interaction

Write out the steps that you believe need to take place before you marry someone. Describe the type of dating relationship you think is biblical.

## Prayer

*Dear Lord, thank you for your Word. I pray for a pure heart, one that will respond appropriately to promises and feelings of love. I know that sex before marriage is a sin, so help me take the right steps in relationships and avoid hurting myself. Please grant me bad-to-the-bone self-control so that I remain a virgin like Rebekah. In Jesus' name I pray, Amen.*

## Memory Verse

Flee sexual immorality. Every sin that a man does is outside the body, but he who commits sexual immorality sins against his own body.

1 Corinthians 6:18

# WEEKEND WARRIOR

## Jether

### Read Judges 8

When I was young, I shared a bedroom with my two brothers. We had the usual brother-type fights, but basically, we had a pretty good time. Our room was your typical guy room. Translation: It smelled like a locker room, probably because of all the games we played there.

One of our favorites was Star Trek. Because I had the top bunk bed, I'd pretend to beam one of my brothers up to the top. When I did, he would have to crawl up between the bed and the wall. One night, my father had had enough of the playing around, and from downstairs yelled his last warning that we should be quiet. My brother begged me not to beam him up. Big mistake. I started to beam him up, and because a rule was a rule, he started to crawl to the top bunk. The closer he got, the louder he laughed (and the closer he got to a whupping). Just then our father walked into the room and found my brother pinned against the wall. Busted. He tried to say that I had forced him up, but it was his decision, and he paid for it.

When God catches you in a sinful act, there's no way you can say that Satan made you do it. You can't be forced to sin. You can always say no and walk away.

Jether practically had this principle tattooed to his forehead. As you read in today's Bible reading, when Jether was challenged by his father, Gideon, to kill the kings of Midian, he did not. Judges 8:20 says, "The youth would not draw his sword; for he was afraid, because he was still a youth." If Jether said no to his father, you can say no to so-called friends who want to bring you down by making you do stuff you shouldn't do.

## Interaction

What do you think you will be challenged to do this weekend that you must be prepared to say no to? Write it down and pray for strength to resist the pressure.

## Prayer

*Dear Lord, thank you for your Word. I pray for the strength and courage to say no to the things you don't want me to do. I pray that I would feel good about not being like everyone else or doing what they want me to do. I only want what you want. Give me the faith to "Just Say No" like Jether. In Jesus' name I pray, Amen.*

# WEEKEND WARRIOR

## Jether

### Read Judges 8

A friend's daughter recently went off to college. After one month, she called me to express her doubts about whether God had called her there. She was lonely and hadn't made any close friends who shared her beliefs. She wanted a word of encouragement.

"What is Satan making you think?" I asked.

"That I'll never find a friend. That I shouldn't be here."

"Well, what's the worst thing that could happen if you don't make any friends this semester?"

She paused a moment, then said, "Nothing, I guess. I'd just go home for Christmas and make sure I saw my old friends."

It was a legitimate desire for this college student to have a close friend and feel at home in a faraway place, but the world wasn't going to end if she didn't find a friend right away. She still had friends from home and church. She still had her family. Satan was just trying to frighten her, making her worry about her college choice.

Satan is a master of making something out of nothing. His favorite weapon is fear. He'll make you scared about things that really don't matter. He'll make you worry what others think about you. He'll make you think that you need to have sex to keep a boyfriend. He'll encourage you to do drugs, drink, steal, or lie.

When Jether was challenged to kill the kings of Midian, it must have been an exciting moment. Think about it, the Midianites had tormented and oppressed the Israelites for over seven years. They had killed Gideon's brothers. But now, after chasing the Midianites over hundreds of miles, Gideon had finally captured their kings. This was a day of great revenge for the people of Israel. Jether could be a hero, the one to actually slay the kings of the enemies.

Still, something inside of Jether told him that he wasn't right for the job. He was young and rightfully scared, but it wasn't Satan tugging at him. Despite the urging of his father, Jether felt that it would be wrong for him to kill the men. He didn't care what his friends would think, nor did he worry about the possible rejection his decision might cause.

Satan will constantly use peer pressure to get you to do things that go against the convictions of your heart. Stick to what you believe the Lord is telling you to do and live by that faith.

## Interaction

Is Satan using fear to try to intimidate you about something? For instance, is he saying you won't be popular unless you get high? Or, you'll make enemies if you don't lie? Write down the one area of life in which Satan is trying to intimidate you. Then look up and list Bible verses that contradict those fears.

## Prayer

*Dear Lord, thank you for your Word. I know that you have not given me the spirit of fear. I know that as your child, I don't need to worry about things. Lord, you know my needs and concerns even before I ask about them. Please give me the patience to wait on you and your direction for my life. I pray that I will never let fear or any other weapon of the Devil entice me into sinning. Give me the faith to "Just Say No" like Jether. In Jesus' name I pray, Amen.*

# WEEK 9

## Be Ready Like Rhoda

The forty years or so after Christ died and rose again was a time of intense persecution against the church. Many Christians were killed for their faith, including the apostle James, brother of John the Baptist. James' death pleased the Jews so much that King Herod had Peter arrested in order to possibly face the same consequences.

It is during this time that we find Rhoda, a bad-to-the-bone girl ready to do whatever God called her to do. This week the Holy Spirit will challenge you to be ready like Rhoda—prepared for intense spiritual battles ahead. May God bless you as you study His Word.

# Memory Verse
# of the Week

Preach the word! Be ready in season and
out of season. Convince, rebuke, exhort,
with all longsuffering and teaching.

2 TIMOTHY 4:2

# MONDAY

## Be First in Line
### Read Acts 12:1–19

I don't know about you, but I hate waiting in lines. And don't even think about cutting in front of me. Nothing irritates me more. At fast-food restaurants I even notice when people come in after me but get their food first. Whether I am standing in line at the movies, in a store, or at the airport, this anxiousness comes from a selfish desire for enjoyment . . . NOW.

All of us are motivated to get what we want, how we want it, and when we want it. But why aren't we like this when it comes to God?

Are you anxious to be blessed? At the front of the line for miracles? It may mean being the first one at the prayer meeting or Bible study, the first to sign up to feed the poor. God wants eager, committed people to do His work.

When Peter was miraculously released from prison, he ran to the house of Mary and knocked on the door. Who was the first one to jump up and answer it? Rhoda. Her actions said, "I want my miracle now." What would you have done when the knock came? Would you have been first in line?

## Interaction

When was the last time you shied away from an opportunity to be used by God? Make a commitment to be first in line the next time He calls for bad-to-the-bone volunteers. Begin praying that God's priorities become your first desires.

## Prayer

*Dear Lord, thank you for your Word. My prayer today is that I will be proactive, not reactive, when it comes to you. I don't want to wait for someone else to do for you what I should be doing. Please prepare me to be first in line like "Ready Rhoda." In Jesus' name I pray, Amen.*

## Memory Verse

Preach the word! Be ready in season and out of season. Convince, rebuke, exhort, with all longsuffering and teaching.

2 Timothy 4:2

# TUESDAY

## Pray for the Impossible

### Read Acts 12:5–13

Peter faced a seemingly impossible situation in prison. He was bound by two chains and flanked between two guards with more guards at the prison doors. Chained and surrounded, how could he possibly escape? Death seemed inevitable. After all, another apostle, James, had already been executed. Most people thought Peter was a goner, but a group of believers refused to give up and instead began to pray for the impossible.

*Peter was therefore kept in prison, but constant prayer was offered to God for him by the church.*

*—Acts 12:5*

And at Mary's house, where many people had gathered to pray for Peter, "Ready Rhoda" was right there, believing for a miracle along with the rest of them.

There will be many times that God will allow you or someone you know to face an impossible situation. The question is, will you be ready for the challenge? What will you do? Will you pray or worry? Will you rejoice or complain? Will you continue to trust God or blame Him?

If you want to be ready like Rhoda, you need to be ready to get on your knees and pray at the first sign of anything impossible. When problems seem insurmountable and life looks grim, put your faith in Matthew 19:26, which says, "With men this is impossible, but with God all things are possible."

### Interaction

Have you stopped praying for a specific "impossible" miracle? Make a commitment today to begin praying like Rhoda that God will come through in a big way and do the impossible.

## Prayer

*Dear Lord, thank you for your Word. I pray that you would grant me the faith to believe that nothing is impossible for you. Give me the faith and the wisdom to pray about everyday things so that when I face the big problems of life I will be bad to the bone and ready like Rhoda. In Jesus' name I pray, Amen.*

## Memory Verse

Preach the word! Be ready in season and out of season. Convince, rebuke, exhort, with all longsuffering and teaching.

2 Timothy 4:2

# WEDNESDAY

## Are You Crazy?

### Read Acts 12:13–19

During a crusade in Mexico with my church, a four-year-old girl with deformed ears was brought to me for prayer. She had an extra ear canal in each ear. With a doctor standing nearby, I had the privilege to pray for the girl's healing. Fifteen minutes later, the doctor called me back to the girl and said her ears were still deformed. However, when I looked she was clearly healed. God had indeed performed a miracle, but because the doctor did not expect a miracle, he was blinded to it.

When Peter knocked at Mary's door and called out to everyone in the house, Rhoda knew it was Peter the moment he spoke. She didn't even open the door. She had prayed for and expected a miracle, and a miracle she got.

At first, nobody believed Rhoda's news about Peter being at the door. They basically said she was crazy. Can you believe it? They called her crazy just because she believed in a miracle. But why were they praying for something they didn't believe could happen? Why were they so shocked when they finally saw Peter?

When God performs a miracle in your life, will you ignore it if Satan and others call you crazy? Or, like Rhoda, will you rebel against criticism and doubts and proclaim God's miracle to everyone? James 1:6 says, "But let him ask in faith with no doubting, for he who doubts is like a wave of the sea driven and tossed by the wind." You must decide whether to believe in God's miracle-making power or doubt it. True faith does not waiver.

### Interaction

A miracle is anything that God does which is impossible for humans to do. Have you ever been the one who did not believe a miracle when it happened? If so, why do you think you doubted? Today, look for a miracle and write it down.

## Prayer

*Dear Lord, thank you for your Word. I pray that I will never limit what you can do in my life. I know that in the past I've said many prayers lacking faith that you would answer them. Please increase my faith in your power. I pray that I would have an expectant heart, looking for miracles in my life. If I have no limits on what you can do, I will be bad to the bone and ready for anything just like Rhoda. In Jesus' name I pray, Amen.*

## Memory Verse

Preach the word! Be ready in season and out of season. Convince, rebuke, exhort, with all longsuffering and teaching.

2 Timothy 4:2

# THURSDAY

## How Well Do You Know Your Pastor?

### Read Acts 12:1–19

They say you should never assume anything, but I'm going to assume that you're part of a church youth group. I also assume that there's a pastor or Bible teacher in your life. Even though you might see these people several times per month, how well do you know them? What do you know about the people who teach you about the Bible? Are you truly being influenced by their lives or are you just listening to them on Sundays? Are you getting everything you can from your relationship with them?

When I'm running around town, I often see people who attend my services each week. Sometimes they recognize me, but other times, unless I say hello or they hear my name, they have no clue who I am.

When Peter came to the door of the house, Rhoda immediately recognized his voice. She and the others had been praying for him. And now she was able to help him to safety.

You may not have a close friendship with your church leaders, but you can still learn from their example. You can still pray for them and their families. Those prayers are critical because Satan wants to destroy your pastor and anyone else who is trying to help you understand and obey the Bible. Get involved in your church. Support the leadership with your prayers. Offer yourself as a servant in the ministry. Increase your interaction with the men and women in leadership beyond simply saying hi and bye on Sundays.

## Interaction

What do you most respect about your pastors or youth leaders? Are these characteristics something you would like to develop in your life? Write down your impressions and begin praying that their admirable characteristics become part of your character.

## Prayer

*Dear Lord, thank you for your Word. I pray that my relationship with my pastor will improve. Help me to learn from his godliness, to follow him as he follows you. When I know your voice and can recognize my pastor's voice, I will be bad to the bone and ready to respond to your call like Rhoda. In Jesus' name I pray, Amen.*

## Memory Verse

Preach the word! Be ready in season and out of season. Convince, rebuke, exhort, with all longsuffering and teaching.

2 Timothy 4:2

# FRIDAY

## Not Scared of You!

### Read Acts 12:1–19

At one of my son's soccer games I got to know the coach's four-year-old son, Matthew. He was just a little guy, but he thought he was a grown man. Over and over he would try to tackle or wrestle me. He probably knew I was harmless, but I couldn't believe his guts.

When the game was over, I thought I'd tease him a bit and try to get him to share his soda.

"Hey, Matthew, give me your drink."

He just laughed and said, "Say it again."

"Give me your drink."

Laughing even louder, he said, "Say it again."

Well, back and forth we went, with him laughing more and more about the game he was playing on me. All I could think was *This little guy is laughing at someone five times his size!*

As children of God, we should laugh at Satan every time he tries to intimidate us. Intimidation is one of Satan's most-used weapons. Even today, if you think about it, you are probably being intimidated into not carrying your Bible to school, witnessing to your friends and classmates, or starting a Christian club.

During Rhoda's lifetime, people were killed for being Christians. James was executed with a sword. Others were fed to lions, crucified upside down, or boiled in oil. It was during this time of threats and intimidation that Rhoda and the other believers dared to have a prayer meeting for Peter. Rhoda had good reason to fear for her life, but she was prepared for the pressure. I can imagine Ready Rhoda staring down death, saying, "Get out of my face." She knew that heaven awaited her if anything bad happened.

What is Satan intimidating you with? The possibility that your beliefs might mean losing some friends? That you'll be known as a Jesus freak? Wow, you're in real danger; someone may make fun of you.

I'm sorry, but you need to stop worrying about what others will think or do if they know you're bad to the bone for Christ. I once heard that eighty percent of what we worry about never happens, and the twenty percent that does occur we can't do anything about. So why worry? Jesus tells us,

*"Therefore do not worry, saying, 'What shall we eat?' or 'What shall we drink?' or 'What shall we wear?' For after all these things the Gentiles seek. For your heavenly Father knows that you need all these things. But seek first the kingdom of God and His righteousness, and all these things shall be added to you."*
*—Matthew 6:31–33*

Make a decision to obey God no matter what consequences you expect.

## Interaction

List the ways Satan can successfully intimidate you. Then write down at least one Bible verse that proves God will overcome that intimidation.

## Prayer

*Dear Lord, thank you for your Word. My prayer today is that I will not be intimidated away from the battle. When I start to worry about things, remind me that you have not given me the spirit of fear. I pray for bad-to-the-bone faith that enables me to laugh at Satan when he tries to intimidate me. In threatening times, help me be ready like Rhoda. In Jesus' name I pray, Amen.*

## Memory Verse

Preach the word! Be ready in season and out of season. Convince, rebuke, exhort, with all longsuffering and teaching.
2 Timothy 4:2

# WEEKEND WARRIOR
## Naaman's Slave Girl
### Read 2 Kings 5:1–14

While on vacation with my family we decided to go fishing. My kids had been asking—no, bugging—me about it for a long time, so we went to a small trout pond and rented poles, and they began to fish.

It didn't take long to see that the fishing wasn't going to be easy. Nobody around us was catching anything, and my kids were spending more time untangling their lines than casting them. An hour had produced only a few nibbles. I had noticed, however, that a trout would come to the surface every two or three minutes to grab a tasty bug dessert. It got me thinking, *I wonder if I could scoop up a fish with our net?* It was worth a shot.

The fishing net only had a three-foot handle, so I sat on a wall with my feet dangling near the water. Sure enough, within five minutes, there it was: a rainbow trout. I reached down into the muddy water, pulled up the net, and lo and behold we had a two-pound keeper.

No matter what your need is today, God is the giver of all good gifts. He is the provider for all our needs. No matter what you are going through, good times or bad, God will not only provide love and encouragement and the necessities for life, but He will provide opportunities for you to serve other people.

In this weekend's Bible reading, the young girl who was taken captive by the Syrian army was given an opportunity to help the people who kidnapped her. Her master, Naaman, had leprosy, and she knew of a man of God called Elijah, who could heal him. So instead of being selfish, instead of whining and complaining about her hard times, she decided to help Naaman.

Are you going through a difficult time right now? One of the important ways that God will encourage you is to give you an opportunity to help someone else who is in need. By helping that person, not only will you be a blessing to that person but you will be blessed in the process. It feels good to help out. It also gets your mind off your own problems. This weekend allow God to show you someone who is in need. Provide encouraging words and share his or her burden. You'll find that it lightens your own load.

## Interaction

Spend time praying for an opportunity to minister to someone else's need, and then write down how good it makes you feel.

## Prayer

*Dear Lord, thank you for your Word. I pray that this weekend you would send someone into my life who has a bigger problem than I do. Send someone into my life who needs my help; someone I can encourage who needs me to bear some of their burden. I pray that in this process you would encourage me. Help me to see that no matter what I am going through, I can always be used by you to help someone else and to build your kingdom. In Jesus' name I pray, Amen.*

# WEEKEND WARRIOR
## Naaman's Slave Girl
### Read 2 Kings 5:1–14

When I was fourteen, a family with three boys bought the house two doors down from us. It had been a long time since anyone new had come to the neighborhood, so on moving day we all stood outside and watched, wondering if the boys were candidates for our street football team.

Right away we could tell there was something different about the three boys. For one thing, they were dressed neatly. On that day and whenever we'd see them later, their clothes were actually coordinated. Let's face it, looking good isn't a priority for most kids. Why bother when you'll rip a hole in your clothes anyway? But these three guys always looked like they were going to Easter service or having their pictures taken. Their pants were creased, their hair greased. How they spoke was also different. All three minded their manners and called adults "sir" or "ma'am." They were always polite and seemed to respect themselves and others. It wasn't hard to see that they had been trained well and had grown up with strict guidelines.

Disciplined training comes in handy during life's difficult times. Without a strong foundation, you will cave in when the pressures of life begin to wear on you. That's why it is very important that you, a young Christian, establish strict guidelines for your attitude and your behavior. These guidelines must direct your life in good times and bad.

In this weekend's Bible reading, the Syrian army kidnapped a young girl and made her a servant. Rather than being angry or depressed, however, she respected her captors and cared for them. When Naaman had leprosy, she looked beyond her misfortune to help him.

When bad things happen to you, what happens to your attitude and outlook on life? This weekend you may be going through difficult times. Take this moment to check and see if your faith and walk with God remain consistent. Proverbs 24:10 says that if you faint in the day of adversity your faith is weak. Are you fainting? Are you losing faith because you're going through adversity?

## Interaction

Write down any trials you're going through right now. How have these difficult times changed your attitude and behavior? Then write down what you believe the Bible says about how you should act and react.

## Prayer

*Dear Lord, thank you for your Word. Thank you for your faithfulness to me. Even when things are going bad, I know that you love me. I know you want me to grow as a Christian. And I know that you will use every incident in my life to help me grow. I pray that I would consistently hold on to your hand and never let the pressures of life choke out my faith and my faithfulness to your Word. In Jesus' name I pray, Amen.*

## Be Discipled Like Samuel

Whenever God needs to get a message to His people, He speaks to those who are loyal to Him and ready to listen. They don't have to be a certain age or hold a fancy position in the church; God speaks to all those who are seeking Him with their hearts and minds. Although God does not always use the sound of a human voice, He always speaks clearly through His Word.

More than one thousand years before Christ was born, God chose and trained a young boy named Samuel to become His main man. At the time, Samuel was being taught or "discipled" by an older priest named Eli. The New King James Version of the Bible describes Samuel as ministering to the Lord *before* Eli. This discipleship prepared Samuel to hear, understand, and obey God—all at a young age.

In order to do good things for God, you will need to follow Samuel's example and find a bad-to-the-bone believer to help you learn about God through a discipleship or mentor relationship. This week you will be challenged to be discipled like Samuel. May God bless you as you study His Word.

# Memory Verse
# of the Week

Be diligent to present yourself approved to
God, a worker who does not need to be
ashamed, rightly dividing the word of truth.

2 TIMOTHY 2:15

# MONDAY

## God's All-Star Team

### Read 1 Samuel 3

Having played football all my life, I can't wait until my son is old enough to hit the gridiron. Until then, soccer is his game. He's a pretty good player, if I do say so myself. In fact, after his first year he tried out for the all-star team. I really wanted him to make it, and sure enough, he was picked for the team and had a great time.

How would you like to be picked for God's all-star team? No, He's not looking for good soccer players. God is assembling the ultimate dream team.

*"For the eyes of the Lord run to and fro throughout the whole earth, to show Himself strong on behalf of those whose heart is loyal to Him."*

—*2 Chronicles 16:9*

And here are the qualifications God desires:

*"Then I will raise up for Myself a faithful priest who shall do according to what is in My heart and in My mind."*

—*1 Samuel 2:35*

Samuel was this sort of person. God prepared Samuel for His all-star team by placing him under the discipleship of Eli, an older, more experienced bad-to-the-bone believer. Eli's discipleship of Samuel served the same function as having a coach in soccer.

Today, God is looking for someone to represent Him in your community—to be on His all-star team. Are you that person?

Having someone to disciple you will help you learn God's perspective in all areas of your life. From Eli, Samuel learned to honor God with his heart, mind, and actions. Samuel honored God with his worship. The best way to learn these things is to be taught by someone who already knows them.

Spend time in prayer, asking God to help you find someone who will teach you about the Lord so that you may know His heart and mind. Perhaps this person has a ministry in which you can serve.

## Interaction

Write down the names of five people you would consider asking to disciple you as a Christian. Ask your parents if there is someone they want you to work with.

## Prayer

*Dear Lord, thank you for your Word. I pray today that I could be picked for your all-star team. As 1 Samuel 2:35 says, you are looking for people who are bad to the bone and seeking your heart and mind. Please raise me as that kind of believer. I know it is important to have someone in my life to train me in your ways. Please give me the desire to be discipled like Samuel. In Jesus' name I pray, Amen.*

## Memory Verse

Be diligent to present yourself approved to God, a worker who does not need to be ashamed, rightly dividing the word of truth.

2 Timothy 2:15

# TUESDAY

## Where Is My Deathbed?

### Read 1 Samuel 3

One evening my family and I were watching TV when a character said something about a man being on his deathbed. My nine-year-old son picked up on the comment, and with a puzzled look on his face asked me, "Dad, how do people know which bed is their deathbed?"

We don't know when or where we will die, I said, but the important thing is to focus on the life God has given us rather than worry about which bed will be our deathbed. In other words, people can either spend their time worrying about dying or they can enjoy living. John 10:10 says, "Jesus has come to give life and give it abundantly." God wants you to have a productive and fruitful life. Being discipled helps gets you to a point where you can experience this abundant life.

This was not the case with Ken. He accepted the Lord in the fall of 1997 but decided that he wanted to live it up a little longer, according to a friend. Ken continued to party and have fun—his way. But then one weekend, during an innocent waterskiing outing, he was hit by a boat and died. Ken's friend came to me in church to ask for prayer and to share this story with me. He said I should use Ken's story to encourage teens not to take God and life for granted.

You never know where your deathbed is. You never know when the end will come. The Bible says that we need to live as though Jesus were returning to earth tonight, because no one knows the hour or the day He will come again (Matthew 24:36). The best way to avoid walking this tightrope is to be sold out for God. You need to be totally consumed by His plan for your life. You need to have His mind and His heart as 1 Samuel 2:35 says,

*"Then I will raise up for Myself a faithful priest who shall do according to what is in My heart and in My mind. I will build him a sure house, and he shall walk before My anointed forever."*

God wants great things from you, but you'll never know when the end will come—where your deathbed will be—so stop putting off until tomorrow what you can do today. God helped prepare Samuel for great things by giving him a teacher, Eli. Ask someone to be your discipler or mentor in the Word of God so that you may become the person God created you to be.

## Interaction

Write down what you would like to learn through a discipleship. Also, describe the type of person you would like your discipler to be, and the nature of the disciple relationship you desire.

## Prayer

*Dear Lord, thank you for your Word. I know that I need to grow and become more committed to your Word. I know that if I had someone to help me, it would be much easier. I pray that I would recognize that teacher, that discipler, when you send him or her into my life. I pray that you would send a bad-to-the-bone believer who has the same heart for my life as you do. Thank you in advance for providing that person. I know that person will be the very thing I need in order to be discipled like Samuel. In Jesus' name I pray, Amen.*

## Memory Verse

Be diligent to present yourself approved to God, a worker who does not need to be ashamed, rightly dividing the word of truth.

2 Timothy 2:15

# WEDNESDAY

## Three . . . Two . . . One
### Read 1 Samuel 3

I was raised in a relatively strict home. We were taught to respect our elders. My father believed in a definite chain of command in the home, with him at the top, and we knew where we stood.

When we'd be out shopping or doing whatever, it used to amaze us to see kids talking back to their parents. We would stop and stare in awe, thinking, *When are they going to get spanked?* Instead, the parents would say things like, "Johnny, if you don't come here by the count of one, you're not going to be able to play later on." The countdown would start: five, four, three, two, one. No change on the part of the kid. Then the parent would warn again, "I want you to come over here by the count of one. Five, four, three, two, one." Same results. Or should I say the same non-results? We couldn't believe it. We had never heard about the count system. Sometimes our father would get so frustrated at what we were witnessing that he would get an attitude and spank *us*.

Don't worry, I'm exaggerating. But the point is, we showed our respect for our dad by how we responded to him. When Dad called us, we responded on the first call. He did not need to call us two or three times. As soon as we heard him we jumped—not out of fear, but respect.

How many times must God call you before you respond? When God called Samuel, the boy jumped up immediately, thinking it was his mentor, Eli. Three times in a row Samuel heard a voice, and three times he jumped up and went to his mentor. Samuel thought, *I'm gonna find out who is calling me, even if I have to get up twenty times.* Finally it was Eli who knew the voice was God's. He told Samuel to respond, "Speak, for your servant hears" (1 Samuel 3:10).

What person in your life directs you to trust in the Lord? Who

163

consistently encourages you and teaches you to look to Jesus for direction and help? This is the kind of person you want your discipler to be.

In addition to finding a bad-to-the-bone discipler who will meet with you on a regular basis, seek out a pastor who teaches the Word in such a way that encourages your Christian growth. Disciplers or mentors don't always have to be someone with whom you spend one-on-one time. They can be someone whose words and life positively impact your life. Begin praying that God would reveal who your discipler should be, and don't be surprised if you already know that someone.

## Interaction

List three people who could consistently encourage you to look to Jesus; people who could disciple you.

## Prayer

*Dear Lord, thank you for your Word. My prayer today is that you would send a bad-to-the-bone discipler into my life who would consistently encourage me to depend on you. I need someone who will point me in your direction every time I need wisdom, love, encouragement, and guidance. I pray that this person would truly fulfill my desire to be discipled like Samuel. In Jesus' name I pray, Amen.*

## Memory Verse

Be diligent to present yourself approved to God, a worker who does not need to be ashamed, rightly dividing the word of truth.
2 Timothy 2:15

# THURSDAY
## In the Word
### Read 1 Samuel 3

You may not realize it, but we live in a time when Christians are not the most popular people around. Our views on abortion, homosexuality, abstinence, and general honesty go against what many people think.

Take time today to listen to what your friends talk about. Try to figure out where they get their opinions and viewpoints. What is the authority behind their understandings and convictions?

In Samuel's time, God rarely spoke to people. 1 Samuel 3:1 says, ". . . the word of the Lord was rare in those days; there was no widespread revelation." Still, even though the whole Bible had not been written yet, people knew God's desires; most simply did not make decisions based on His will. Samuel, on the other hand, rebelled against the rest of society. He was the one who decided to trust in the Word of God and God's voice.

Make a decision today to be a man or woman of God's Word. Make a decision today to begin memorizing a Scripture verse or passage each week. Make a decision today to base your opinions on what the Bible says and teaches. Make a decision today that your behavior will reflect God's heart and mind.

For starters, memorize Psalm 119:9–11 this week. It promises that if you obey God's Word, He will purify your way.

*How can a young man cleanse his way? By taking heed according to Your word. With my whole heart I have sought You; Oh, let me not wander from Your commandments! Your word I have hidden in my heart, that I might not sin against You!*

# Interaction

List four verses that you will memorize this month. Make a commitment to memorize one per week.

# Prayer

*Dear Lord, thank you for your Word. My prayer today is that I would become a bad-to-the-bone disciple of your Word. Plant your Word in my heart. Give me a desire to memorize and live your Word. Give me the ability to think of Bible verses when I am walking, running, talking with friends, and doing my homework. May I meditate on your Word day and night. Please send someone who can hold me accountable to consistently memorizing your Word. Please send someone to help me that I may truly be discipled like Samuel. In Jesus' name I pray, Amen.*

# Memory Verse

Be diligent to present yourself approved to God, a worker who does not need to be ashamed, rightly dividing the word of truth.

2 Timothy 2:15

# FRIDAY

## God's Place

### Read 1 Samuel 3

The mobile phone has to be one of the biggest time-saving inventions ever. It's so convenient to be able to talk to anyone from anywhere: while driving, walking in the mall, or hanging out in the park with my kids. Despite the convenience of mobile phones, I've learned that there are certain places near my home where the reception is always terrible and other places where I get a clear connection. For important calls, I go to the good spots so I can hear and be heard clearly.

When Samuel first heard a voice calling to him, he did not know it was God's voice. Samuel kept going to his mentor, Eli, and asking if it was Eli who was calling him. After the third time, Samuel finally figured out that the voice was God's.

> *Therefore Eli said to Samuel, "Go, lie down; and it shall be, if He calls you, that you must say, 'Speak, Lord, for Your servant hears.'" So Samuel went and lay down in his place.*
> *—1 Samuel 3:9*

Where do you go when you want to hear God clearly? Samuel had a "place" where he heard God. Where is yours? Is it your bedroom, the yard, balcony, school library, a nearby park?

Hearing God involves more than finding the perfect geographical place, it means making sure you are in the right "place" mentally, emotionally, and spiritually. How do you prepare your heart, mind, and soul to hear and receive God's Word? Pray for a receptive, humble heart that you may be able to accept God's will for your life.

## Interaction

Write down the one place where you can regularly spend at least fifteen minutes a day listening and talking to God. It should be quiet and private; a place where you can listen for and hear the voice of God daily.

## Prayer

*Dear Lord, thank you for your Word. I want to hear your voice clearly each day. I need direction and encouragement that only you can provide. Please show me where I should go to hear you and give me bad-to-the-bone discipline to get there every day. Please help me set strict spiritual guidelines in my life so that I may live the life of someone who is discipled like Samuel. In Jesus' name I pray, Amen.*

## Memory Verse

Be diligent to present yourself approved to God, a worker who does not need to be ashamed, rightly dividing the word of truth.

2 Timothy 2:15

# WEEKEND WARRIOR
## Jonathan's Lad
### Read 1 Samuel 20

Every time I see Matt, a local youth pastor, he has a member of his youth group with him. He tries to involve young people in most everything he does, from running errands or visiting a sick kid to shopping for supplies for a church event or simply hanging out. This practice is very useful in training disciples because it exposes them to many different experiences. Matt also uses the time together to teach the importance of obedience. No matter what the task, if the young person wants to grow, he or she must be submissive and cannot complain.

In this weekend's Bible reading, Jonathan (King Saul's son) and David devised a scheme to save David's life. Jonathan told David to hide in the woods and wait for a secret message. If Jonathan told a "lad" to fetch arrows from a certain place, David could safely return to the palace. If the arrows were shot beyond David's hiding place, David should run for his life. As you read, everything went as planned. David fled and escaped certain death—thanks in large part to the teenage boy who fetched the arrows without complaining or questioning his mission. This teenager wanted nothing but to get the job done. When he was told to get the arrows, he responded as if saying, "Get out of my way, people, I have to go!" He just obeyed. Jonathan did not have time or the liberty to explain the situation. He needed someone who would simply serve, and without an argument.

If you are going to learn from someone, you will need to just do what you are told. You must learn to be a submissive, humble servant.

### Interaction

This weekend make a point to volunteer your services to an adult. Promise yourself that you'll serve with a humble heart, without a complaint or argument. Be supportive and encouraging.

## Prayer

*Dear Lord, thank you for your Word. I pray that I will learn to serve with a humble heart like Jonathan's lad. I pray that I would be submissive to those who teach me how to be a servant and disciple. May I become the servant you need in your kingdom. In Jesus' name I pray, Amen.*

# WEEKEND WARRIOR

## Jonathan's Lad

### Read 1 Samuel 20:35–40

t's cool how the small things in life often make a huge difference. When we were making a video for one of our crusades, we discovered a young teenager with an incredible story. Aaron was brought to a crusade by a friend who was walking strong with God after receiving Him a year earlier. The friend knew Aaron did not know the Lord and needed to be saved. However, the friend had no clue that Aaron had been thinking about killing himself. Aaron felt that his life was going nowhere and that no one would even miss him if he died. But when Aaron went to the crusade and heard the music and the message, he realized that it was Jesus he was looking for. When the altar call was made, he came forward and gave his life to Jesus Christ. The friend's simple invitation had truly saved Aaron's earthly and eternal life.

When I was a youth pastor, most kids gladly helped out in ministry. But every now and then, someone would question why I wanted him or her to do something. They'd basically ask, "What's in it for me?"

In this weekend's Bible reading, the young man never asked Jonathan, "Why don't you fetch your own arrows?" He simply did his job, never even realizing how important it was.

When you serve in God's army, you will probably never know how many young people your help will affect. In God's kingdom, everything has eternal importance. Every person and every job is significant to God. Matthew 25:23 says, "His lord said to him, 'Well done, good and faithful servant; you have been faithful over a few things, I will make you ruler over many things. Enter into the joy of your lord.' "

When you are faithful in the little things, God can trust you with bigger things.

## Interaction

Write down one instance when you thought that what you did mattered very little, only to later find out that it changed a life. If you can't think of one, make a commitment to do something for God today, something of eternal significance.

## Prayer

*Dear Lord, thank you for your Word. I pray that today you would use me in a life-changing experience. I want to be a servant who makes a difference in someone's life. I want to help others grow closer to you. May I commit at least one totally unselfish act today on behalf of someone else. In Jesus' name I pray, Amen.*

# WEEK 11

# Be Bold Like Shadrach, Meshach, and Abed-Nego

Have you ever been asked to do something that is clearly against what the Bible teaches? Maybe you've been pressured by kids at school to drink or do drugs.

This week you will get to better know three teenagers who faced the highest degree of peer pressure possible; the king of the entire known world commanded them to bow to his idol or die by fire. As you will read, Shadrach, Meshach, and Abed-Nego did not bow. Instead, they took a stand and were bold until the end.

If they had what it took to withstand such intense peer pressure, imagine how their techniques could help you deal with the pressures you face every day. This week the Holy Spirit will challenge you to be bold to stand like Shadrach, Meshach, and Abed-Nego. May God bless you as you study His Word.

# Memory Verse
# of the Week

"Do not fear those who kill the body but cannot kill the soul. But rather fear Him who is able to destroy both soul and body in hell."

MATTHEW 10:28

# MONDAY

## Want to Be Promoted?

### Read Daniel 1:3–20; 2:49

While filming a video about gangs, I asked gang members some rapid-fire questions about the "benefits" of gang life. If I joined their gang . . .

Would I have to get beat up by them to prove myself? *Yes*, they answered.

Would my chances of getting arrested increase? *Yes*.

Would my chances of becoming a target of rival gangs go up? *Yes*.

Would my chances of doing drugs and committing crimes increase? *Yes*.

Then I turned up the heat:

If a young person decided to not join and resist gang involvement, would the gang eventually leave that person alone and respect his or her decision? *Yes*, they reluctantly said.

Would that person eventually have every chance to succeed in life? *Yes*.

In the long run, would that person be better off by not being in a gang? *Yes*.

By the time we ended the interview, the gang members had admitted that there were no long-term benefits to gang life. In fact, only prison and death lay ahead.

You may not be pressured to join a gang, but almost every young person is pressured to join a crowd that does things that don't meet God's approval. Drinking, drugs, and other risky activities will eventually destroy you, just as surely as life in a gang.

In today's Bible reading, we see that Shadrach, Meshach, and Abed-Nego learned early on that following the crowd would never get them ahead in life as quickly and safely as joining God. Along with Daniel, these three bad-to-the-bone young men decided not to defile themselves with the king's food and wine and God rewarded them for their loyalty.

*As for these four young men, God gave them knowledge and skill in all literature and wisdom; and Daniel had understanding in all visions and dreams. . . . Then the king interviewed them, and among them all none was found like Daniel, [Shadrach, Meshach, and Abed-Nego]; therefore they served before the king. And in all matters of wisdom and understanding about which the king examined them, he found them ten times better than all the magicians and astrologers who were in all his realm.*

*—Daniel 1:17, 19–20*

Because Daniel, Shadrach, Meshach, and Abed-Nego followed God by faith and resisted what they thought was wrong, they were promoted above all the others who submitted to the king's pressure.

## Interaction

What gang or crowd are you under pressure to join? What "fun" and "happiness" are they promising you? Today, if you feel pressured to follow the crowd, identify the false promises they make. Then, through prayer and the reading of God's Word, ask God to meet your needs.

## Prayer

*Dear Lord, thank you for your Word. My prayer today is to always remember that only you can get me ahead in life. I realize that though the crowd may promise fun and happiness, only you can deliver true satisfaction and contentment in life. Please strengthen me so that I do not let others intimidate and ridicule me. I want to be bold like Shadrach, Meshach, and Abed-Nego. In Jesus' name I pray, Amen.*

## Memory Verse

"Do not fear those who kill the body but cannot kill the soul. But rather fear Him who is able to destroy both soul and body in hell."

Matthew 10:28

# TUESDAY

## Make a Commitment Not to Bow

### Read Daniel 3

One of the most frustrating things I do is counsel teen couples who have just found out that they're pregnant. Among other things, we discuss the events that led up to the pregnancy. After looking at each other and trying to avoid the topic, they usually say they just found themselves in a situation they couldn't handle. Sorry, but that answer won't get them off the hook or help prevent another pregnancy.

Every day, Satan is going to put many temptations in your path. If you are going to resist his sinful ways, you must be prepared. Before leaving your house, make a commitment that you are not going to bow to temptation or peer pressure.

Shadrach, Meshach, and Abed-Nego became marked men when they were promoted by Nebuchadnezzar. Jealous people tried to make them bow to and worship a false idol that resembled Nebuchadnezzar. As the music played, they were told to bow to the idol or else. Under the threat of being thrown into a fiery furnace, they refused to follow the crowd. But how? Did they decide right there on the spot? No, their quick response revealed that they knew well before the ceremony what they would do. No matter what temptation they faced, they would never bow or give in.

Today and every day you must decide that no matter what idols or temptations the Devil may throw in your face, you won't bow—you won't cave in. This commitment must be made before the actual temptation comes.

## Interaction

List the number one temptation or idol that you want to be bold to stand against today.

## Prayer

*Dear Lord, thank you for your Word. My prayer today is that before getting off my knees I will make and keep a commitment not to bow to temptations and false idols. I realize Satan's temptations are strong and I need to prepare myself now to resist them. I pray that I could be bad-to-the-bone bold to stand like Shadrach, Meshach, and Abed-Nego. In Jesus' name I pray, Amen.*

## Memory Verse

"Do not fear those who kill the body but cannot kill the soul. But rather fear Him who is able to destroy both soul and body in hell."

Matthew 10:28

# WEDNESDAY
## Closer Than a Brother
### Read Daniel 3

When I was in high school, I had to be taken to the hospital twice for stitches—once in my foot and the other for a head injury. Both times my friend Mike was there for me.

A truly close friend, according to Proverbs 18:24, is someone who "sticks closer than a brother." Mike was that kind of friend. We stuck together through good and bad times. And the best way to get such a friend is found in the first part of the same verse: "A man who has friends must himself be friendly."

Shadrach, Meshach, and Abed-Nego hung together through thick and thin. When they were being pressured to bow to King Nebuchadnezzar's idol, they kept each other faithful and strong. They undoubtedly encouraged each other through the pressures that threatened their lives. If one had shown signs of weakness, he could depend on the boldness of the other two to hold him up. They fired each other up when the situation got hot—literally. They got in each other's faces and said, "Yo, man, don't forget the commitment we made to God that we would never ever bow."

If you think about it, I'm sure you have friends who are struggling with some sort of temptation in their lives. They have fallen in some way and need encouragement. As a faithful friend, you can help your friends stay faithful to God. James 5:20 lets us know that "he who turns a sinner from the error of his way will save a soul from death and cover a multitude of sins."

## Interaction

List three things you can do to be a better friend.

## Prayer

*Dear Lord, thank you for your Word. My prayer today is that I would find one friend who can help keep me accountable and bold to stand against peer pressure. I know that to have friends I must be friendly. Teach me to be that kind of friend. Please send someone into my life and give us a dependable friendship that will hold strong through thick and thin. I pray for a reliable bad-to-the-bone friend who will help me be bold to stand like Shadrach, Meshach, and Abed-Nego. In Jesus' name I pray, Amen.*

## Memory Verse

"Do not fear those who kill the body but cannot kill the soul. But rather fear Him who is able to destroy both soul and body in hell."

Matthew 10:28

# THURSDAY
## Holy Limits
### Read Daniel 3

At a church picnic some time ago I found myself in the middle of a family tug-of-war. The grandmother of three teens asked me if I thought she should allow them to go out to the movies. She didn't want them exposed to the junk in so many movies. She also did not want them to listen to the music that other teens loved or to watch certain TV shows. The grandchildren, on the other hand, asked me if she was being extreme.

Whenever I'm asked questions that place me in the middle of two opinions, I try to answer in the manner Jesus would—with another question.

"Do you know why your grandma doesn't want you to see those movies and TV shows or listen to that music?"

Reluctantly they admitted, "Because one compromise would lead to another."

Good answer, but they still weren't off the hook. "How holy do you want to be?"

Shadrach, Meshach, and Abed-Nego would not even save their lives by bowing because they knew it would lead to more compromises in their walk with the Lord. Think about it—they were not being asked to kill or rob someone. All they had to do was bow to some golden image. But they knew that if they gave Satan one inch, he would take a mile. So when the opportunity to bow came upon the young men, they looked at one another and said, "Not one inch, dude, not one inch."

Bad-to-the-bone boldness begins with resisting the small things. Satan knows that if he can get you to compromise your integrity in a small issue, then he can slowly get you to compromise in bigger and bigger issues. Soon you will find yourself doing destructive things you once vowed never to do.

## Interaction

List three areas in your life that you are bending the rules to do (laughing at inappropriate jokes; watching TV shows or listening to music that you know doesn't honor God). Make these areas of struggle off limits.

## Prayer

*Dear Lord, thank you for your Word. My prayer today is that I would not bow to even the small temptations. Lord, I pray that I will be bad to the bone and recognize Satan's idols that he places in my life. Help me remember that if I bow once, I will bow twice. I pray that I will be bold like Shadrach, Meshach, and Abed-Nego. In Jesus' name I pray, Amen.*

## Memory Verse

"Do not fear those who kill the body but cannot kill the soul. But rather fear Him who is able to destroy both soul and body in hell."

Matthew 10:28

# FRIDAY
## Peer Pressure
### Read Daniel 3

As a freshman, Todd was trying his best to make friends at his new high school. He thought it would be a good idea to go to a party at the home of a senior. When he got there the music was pumping and everyone was partying just like he expected, but there was also a group of kids into something he did not want to be involved in—drugs. It wasn't long before an upperclassman came over and offered him some free cocaine. Todd had to make a decision: say *no* like his parents taught him, or get high with the other kids.

You'd probably say this is a classic case of peer pressure. But what is peer pressure? I say it's being influenced and pressured by the people you fear disappointing the most. In this story, who does Todd want to avoid disappointing the most? His parents, or kids he barely knows?

When Shadrach, Meshach, and Abed-Nego were told to bow to Nebuchadnezzar's idol, they had to decide who they wanted to avoid disappointing the most, the king or God. Of course, their actions sent a loud message: Sorry, my brother. You may be the king, but we would rather let you down than God.

Each time you feel peer pressure, ask yourself who you would disappoint the most. One way to help you decide is to weigh the consequences of disappointing those around you. Your peers can and will get over it. If you disappoint so-called friends, you can make new ones. Look around your school. More than likely there are a lot of kids who believe what you believe and will not ask you to do anything that could harm you.

If you disappoint your parents, you will create daily stress in your family. Remember, these are the people who brought you into the world. They have clothed, fed, and housed you all your life. Your family members are probably the only people who will be part of your life for your entire life.

If you disappoint God, you sin, and the penalty is death to your joy, peace, and self-control. It will result in nothing good. You will miss out on enjoying the abundant life He has promised you. You will cheat yourself out of the blessings that come from walking with and pleasing Him.

## Interaction

List three areas that peer pressure is tempting you to do something wrong. As you consider these areas of temptation, are you trying not to disappoint people who really don't matter?

## Prayer

*Dear Lord, thank you for your Word. My prayer today is that my consistent boldness to stand against peer pressure will earn me the title Servant of the Most High God. I pray that I would always fear disappointing you, Lord, more than anyone else. I pray that loving, obeying, and listening to you would be more important than following my peers. I realize that you are my most reliable friend. Please give me bad-to-the-bone strength to be bold like Shadrach, Meshach, and Abed-Nego and to stand against peer pressure. In Jesus' name I pray, Amen.*

## Memory Verse

"Do not fear those who kill the body but cannot kill the soul. But rather fear Him who is able to destroy both soul and body in hell."

Matthew 10:28

# WEEKEND WARRIOR
## The Boy Who Fed Thousands
### Read John 6:1–14

It was during the Passover feast, when millions of people were walking to Jerusalem to make sacrifices at the temple, that Jesus decided to preach a sermon to a group of about five thousand. After He finished teaching, He saw that the people were hungry and asked the disciples to feed them. When they realized there was no food, they didn't know what to do. Then one of his disciples told him about a young boy in the crowd.

*"There is a lad here who has five barley loaves and two small fish, but what are they among so many?"*

—*John 6:9*

They asked the little boy to give up his food in order to feed the people. Think about it—the only thing this kid had were five loaves of bread and two fish, and Jesus was going to try to feed five thousand people with it? The boy must have thought, *What difference will my food make?*

How often have you thought, *I don't have anything that would make a difference in God's kingdom*? Have you wondered what difference a single prayer, an apology, feeding a homeless person, or reading a chapter from the Bible each morning makes? Here's the answer: It's totally up to God.

When the boy gave his bread to Christ, He prayed over it and fed more than five thousand people. You never know how far God can multiply your talents, gifts, or prayers. It's not up to you to decide what impact you or something you do can have on someone. You are simply to surrender and submit your life and things to the Lord. The Bible says that you belong to God and that He bought you with a price.

*For you were bought at a price; therefore glorify God in your body and in your spirit, which are God's.*

*—1 Corinthians 6:20*

Everything you have—everything about you—belongs to God. So today, make a decision not to act based on what you think the outcome may be. Your master has needs of you. Don't hold back anything from God, because what you hold back, He will not bless.

## Interaction

What talents, gifts, or resources are you holding back from God? Write them down and then next to them write, "Dear God, I surrender this to you. Use it in any way you want. By faith, I believe that you can bless it and multiply it better than I can. Please do that. Your faithful servant, _____."

## Prayer

*Dear Lord, thank you for your Word. I pray that I will never limit what I think you can do with my talents. I want this so much that I pray for the faith to dream big when it comes to multiplying my talents. I need to be able to think like you think. Lord, please maximize the use of what you have given me. In Jesus' name I pray, Amen.*

# WEEKEND WARRIOR
## The Boy Who Fed Thousands
### Read John 6:1–14

One day I bought each of my children a bag of candy. When I got home, I handed out the bags. But after they had begun eating, I realized that I had mixed up the bags, so I asked them to return them to me. I didn't know it at first, but my daughter kept some of her candy before returning the bag to me. She didn't think I would replace the bag with something better.

Isn't this what we do to God when we hold back our best from Him? We don't believe that God will bless us with something better than what we have?

In this weekend's Bible story, the best thing the boy did was to surrender everything to the Lord. When Jesus asked, the boy gave. He did not hold back one bit. As a result, God blessed all the bread and fish and used it for His glory.

God has asked you for your life—all of your talents, dreams, and desires. He wants to use them and bless them for His glory. Imagine how good of a preacher, teacher, prayer warrior, worship leader, or servant you would be if God had total control of all your talents. Imagine how far He could stretch your money if He had total control of your paycheck. And imagine the beautiful relationship you would have with a boyfriend or girlfriend if you would let Him bring them to you. All this is possible if you let God have it all. But if you hold some back, you are telling Him you only want a partial blessing.

If you decide to hold something back from God, what will you do with it? Do you really think you can make better use of it than Him? Certainly not. Decide today that you will surrender everything to God.

## Interaction

List the talents you have that need to be surrendered to God and used for His glory. Make a commitment to give them fully to Him.

## Prayer

*Dear Lord, thank you for the incredible promise to use me. I want to be used to your fullest potential. May I be part of your plan today to save someone's life for the good of your kingdom. In Jesus' name I pray, Amen.*

## Be Faithful Like Timothy

I praise God for all of the young people who are raised in the church. They learn at an early age to walk with God. Sadly, some fall away from that relationship and begin to rebel against God.

Timothy was raised and nurtured by a godly mother and grandmother. He grew up learning the Word of God and worshiping and serving Him. Best of all, when this young man got older he didn't drift away from God like some people. Timothy held on to the apostle Paul's words:

> You must continue in the things which you have learned and been assured of, knowing from whom you have learned them, and that from childhood you have known the Holy Scriptures, which are able to make you wise for salvation through faith which is in Christ Jesus.
>
> —2 Timothy 3:14–15

This solid foundation came in handy when God called Timothy into the ministry. Timothy was faithful in the little things that God later used for big things. This week you will study Timothy's bad-to-the-bone childhood and how it affected his adult ministry. You will be challenged to be faithful like Timothy. May God bless you as you study His Word.

# Memory Verse
## of the Week

Not that I have already attained, or am
already perfected; but I press on, that I
may lay hold of that for which Christ Jesus
has also laid hold of me.

PHILIPPIANS 3:12

# MONDAY

## Look What I Got

### Read 2 Timothy 1

I was visiting a Christian school and speaking in the chapel when I noticed a small disturbance in the back of the room. A group of guys had been talking, and a teacher grabbed one of the kids and escorted him outside. After my talk, school officials asked if I would speak to the young man who had caused the commotion. As we walked to see the student, the counselor began telling me about the trouble the boy had been in. He frequently cut class and had been caught smoking and also cheating on exams—relatively minor problems but serious enough to risk getting expelled.

At first the boy did not want to even look at me, but he eventually opened up. As we talked, he began to tell me about all the stress and pressure he was under. He then began to blame his dad for all his problems. Apparently the man had left the family, and now the boy's mom was raising him on her own.

As the boy talked about his life, I couldn't help thinking, *This is not a good enough excuse to justify or explain the things you've done. There are countless kids who don't have a dad or mom at home, and they've stayed out of trouble.*

Timothy's own father did not believe in God.

*Then [Paul] came to Derbe and Lystra. And behold, a certain disciple was there, named Timothy, the son of a certain Jewish woman who believed, but his father was Greek [a nonbeliever].*
*—Acts 16:1*

Timothy's mother and grandmother were the spiritual leaders of the home. Paul writes in 2 Timothy 1:5 that he is filled with joy "when I call to remembrance the genuine faith that is in you, which dwelt first in your grandmother Lois and your mother Eunice, and I am persuaded is in you also."

Instead of complaining and blaming other people for what you don't have, start praising God for what you do have. Timothy may not have had a father who believed in God, but he had two godly women in his life who made the whole difference. Timothy was the kind of person who did not look back and complain but pressed forward to claim victory in God's name.

Who do you have in your life right now that you need to begin praising God for? God has probably placed someone in your life to help and encourage you, but you can't see it.

## Interaction

List the names of people you haven't appreciated enough. Make a commitment to pray for those who are positioned to help your spiritual growth.

## Prayer

*Dear Lord, thank you for your Word. I pray for bad-to-the-bone faith to take full advantage of the opportunities, resources, and people you have put into my life in order that I may grow into the Christian you want me to be. Lord, I pray that I could be faithful like Timothy. In Jesus' name I pray, Amen.*

## Memory Verse

Not that I have already attained, or am already perfected; but I press on, that I may lay hold of that for which Christ Jesus has also laid hold of me.

Philippians 3:12

# TUESDAY

## Pray for Me

### Read 2 Timothy 1

E very week at a service I lead at Horizon Christian Fellowship in San Diego, I look forward to seeing Keith, a seven-year-old who sits in the front row with his mom. After the service, he always walks over to me to say hi and get a hug.

One Sunday Keith told me that he had prayed for me the previous night. I then asked him to pray for me every day. I asked him to pray that I would have wisdom and power. I told him that I'd pray for him, too. Since then, when I see Keith, I make a point to ask if he's still praying for me. He's pretty shy, so he usually just smiles, leaving his mom to tell me if he's prayed for me.

Timothy had two faithful people praying for him—his mom and grandmother. Timothy lived with BIG-TIME confidence and faith because he knew that prayers were made on his behalf. He knew that God was hearing his name daily through prayer. But Timothy did not leave it there. He also prayed. He was committed to living according to the prayers being said for him.

Who is praying for you? Chances are your mom, grandmother, a youth leader, or someone in your church is praying for you. Often, people around you will recognize before you do ways in which you need prayer. But I also suggest that you specifically ask others to pray for you. Be sure to let them know what they should pray for, whether it relates to school or work situations or general spiritual growth.

What do you think are the top two things that people are praying about for your life? You can empower these prayers in three ways: First, pray the same thing for yourself; second, make a commitment to live according to those prayers; third, thank people for their prayers and encourage them to continue to pray.

## Interaction

Who do you think is praying for you? Talk to these people, find out what they are praying for, and then put into practice the three prayer-empowerment steps mentioned above.

## Prayer

*Dear Lord, thank you for your Word. I pray that today I will begin to appreciate the prayers that other people are offering up to you on my behalf. I pray that I would show that appreciation by agreeing with their prayer requests as well as making a commitment to live out those prayers in my daily life. I know I desperately need these prayers to remain bad to the bone and faithful like Timothy. In Jesus' name I pray, Amen.*

## Memory Verse

Not that I have already attained, or am already perfected; but I press on, that I may lay hold of that for which Christ Jesus has also laid hold of me.

Philippians 3:12

# WEDNESDAY

## Real Wisdom

### Read 2 Timothy 3

There was a time when my wife and I looked into and even began homeschooling our children. In seminars and conferences, we heard many homeschooling success stories. But the number one question that nagged me was, How do you know what to teach? With all the possible subjects and education requirements these days, how do you make sure your kids don't fall behind kids attending traditional schools? The most common answer: Teach kids the Bible; if they can come to learn, respect, and love God's Word, they will be good students.

Proverbs 1:7 says, "The fear of the Lord is the beginning of knowledge, but fools despise wisdom and instruction." To fear the Lord is to respect Him as God. When this happens, you are enabled to receive from Him real wisdom and understanding. And because wisdom is the correct use of knowledge, with it you will be able to use the information you have in the correct way.

Timothy was faithful in learning and obeying the Bible lessons he had as a young man. He was one of those bad-to-the-bone Church Boyz who prayed for the kids who were in trouble because they lacked wisdom. Whenever Timothy had to confront someone, he used God's Word to "slice and dice 'em up." If he had to make a decision, God's Word was at his side. And God used this Bible knowledge and spiritual wisdom in Timothy's ministry. Paul told Timothy,

*You must continue in the things which you have learned and been assured of, knowing from whom you have learned them, and that from childhood you have known the Holy Scriptures, which are*

*able to make you wise for salvation through faith which is in Christ Jesus.*

*—2 Timothy 3:14–15*

All of us have many opportunities to learn the Bible. In addition to reading the Bible on our own, we can learn more about God's Word during church services and in Bible classes, through devotionals like this one, and many more ways. Take advantage of them all to receive all you can from the Bible.

## Interaction

List and then take advantage of the many opportunities you have to learn God's Word.

## Prayer

*Dear Lord, thank you for your Word. I pray today that I will be faithful like Timothy by faithfully learning, respecting, and obeying your Word. I believe the words of Proverbs 1:7, which says, "The fear of the Lord is the beginning of knowledge, but fools despise wisdom and instruction." I pray for bad-to-the-bone discipline and faith to trust in your Word rather than leaning on my own understanding. I pray that I can take advantage of every opportunity to grow and be faithful like Timothy. In Jesus' name I pray, Amen.*

## Memory Verse

Not that I have already attained, or am already perfected; but I press on, that I may lay hold of that for which Christ Jesus has also laid hold of me.

Philippians 3:12

# THURSDAY

## Be an Example

### Read 1 Timothy 4:12–16

I love it when sports figures and other famous people are interviewed about their personal lives. I want to hear how they made it to the top; about their struggles and how they overcame them. When Timothy was a young man, he had the big responsibility of overseeing a church in Ephesus. He had to confront problems in the church and risk resistance from older members. For many, this challenge would be too big to handle, but Timothy had Paul's support—and advice. "You're the Man," Paul said. "Now act like it." He told Timothy to be on the offensive, to use all the gifts and talents God had given him for the job.

*Let no one despise your youth, but be an example to the believers in word, in conduct, in love, in spirit, in faith, in purity.*
*—1 Timothy 4:12*

Never be intimidated because of your age to speak God's truth to anyone. You are God's child, a chosen vessel. If someone shuts you down because of your age, in a very spiritual, loving, and gentle way, tell them to BACK OFF! Then pray for them.

### Interaction

From today's Bible reading, list all the things Paul told Timothy to do. Make a commitment to begin practicing these actions in your own life.

### Prayer

*Dear Lord, thank you for your word. I pray today that I will be a positive example to all believers, both younger and older than me.*

*I pray that I would identify my gifts and calling and perfect them.
I don't ever want to let my age be a hindrance to how you use me.
I pray that I can be bad to the bone and faithful like Timothy. In
Jesus' name I pray, Amen.*

## Memory Verse

Not that I have already attained, or am already perfected; but I
press on, that I may lay hold of that for which Christ Jesus has
also laid hold of me.

Philippians 3:12

# FRIDAY

## Keep the Main Thing the Main Thing

### Read the verses listed in today's text

Several years ago, on a trip to New York to see family, my father drove me and my wife and child to the airport. As we were saying good-bye, he looked at the birthmark on my hand. (I have a discoloration that begins on the tip of my finger and runs the length of my arm and onto my neck.) He didn't tell me at the time, but he later revealed that he experienced a flood of memories at that moment.

He began to remember the boy who had played little league baseball. The boy who wore a suit to private school and a smelly robe around the house the rest of the day. Now that little boy was grown up and had a family of his own. Those precious days were nothing but a memory. As he reflected on those things he began to realize how much he loved me. He told me that he sobbed during the entire twenty-minute drive home. His heart bore witness to the importance of family. He realized how fast his life and mine had passed by. He was happy that his little boy had grown up to be a dad and husband.

What kind of adult will you become? It's all up to you, but if you are faithful like Timothy and follow Paul's advice to the young minister, you'll have the right priorities in life. You'll keep the main thing the main thing.

Timothy was told by Paul to be faithful in many things like church discipline and doctrine, taking care of widows, not letting anyone despise his youth, and opposing false teaching (1 Timothy 1:3–7, 18–20; 6:3–5, 20–21). Paul warned against perilous times that are to come (2 Timothy 3:1–9). He urged Timothy to follow his example (2 Timothy 3:10–13). But the most important piece of advice was to be faithful in fighting only

God's battles. Paul encouraged Timothy to be bad to the bone and faithful by keeping his eyes on God's battles, not man's.

*This charge I commit to you, son Timothy, according to the prophecies previously made concerning you, that by them you may wage the good warfare, having faith and a good conscience, which some having rejected, concerning the faith have suffered shipwreck.*
—1 Timothy 1:18–19

Life is not about quick success or becoming rich overnight. It is about being faithful over the long term. Chill out and get the job done. Don't worry about unimportant things, just be happy and stay faithful to God. My prayer is that you would have the mindset of Timothy to keep the main thing the main thing.

## Interaction

Look up the word *faithful* in a dictionary and write down the definition. Then make a commitment to live that definition as it pertains to the things of God.

## Prayer

*Dear Lord, thank you for your Word. I pray that I would not try to take shortcuts through life. Please give me the wisdom and discipline to be faithful in the little but important areas of life, trusting that your way is always the best way for me. I pray that in all areas of my personal development I can be faithful like Timothy. In Jesus' name I pray, Amen.*

## Memory Verse

Not that I have already attained, or am already perfected; but I press on, that I may lay hold of that for which Christ Jesus has also laid hold of me.

Philippians 3:12

# WEEKEND WARRIOR
## Manasseh
### Read 2 Chronicles 33:1–11

One of my biggest disappointments as a youth pastor is running into former students who have drifted from the Lord. When I knew them best, they attended my Bible studies week after week, year after year, hearing the Gospel over and over again. They memorized verses, were discipled in the Word, and participated in evangelistic outreaches and missionary trips.

But for some reason now, they've walked away from a godly life. They are three, five, ten years older but no more wiser. They are living according to the world's directions and doing things the Bible says are wrong.

Manasseh was this kind of kid. He became king at the age of twelve and reigned with his godly dad, Hezekiah, for about a decade. For those ten years he was exposed to the godly influence of his dad. He saw how to be a good king and leader. But for some reason it didn't impact the way Manasseh would be king. The Bible says that he reversed what his dad had done.

> For he rebuilt the high places which Hezekiah his father had bro-
> ken down; he raised up altars for the Baals, and made wooden
> images; and he worshipped all the host of heaven and served
> them. He also built altars in the house of the Lord, of which the
> Lord had said, "In Jerusalem shall My name be forever."
> —2 Chronicles 33:3–4

Being around godly people and having godly friends and parents does not guarantee you'll end up godly. If you are determined to be a knuck-lehead, that's what you'll be. But if you decide to pursue godliness, that's what you'll get.

This weekend make a decision about what kind of Christian you want to be now and when you grow up. A lifelong walk with the Lord is not automatic; it's a result of actively deciding to get the most out of the godly people in your life. Don't let a good opportunity pass you by as you ignore the good influence of others. You may not know it, but these people are answers to your prayers. They can teach and counsel you; they can comfort your pain. Reject the help God has sent your way and you will be held accountable.

## Interaction

Who are the godly people in your life? You may not be able to spend much time with every godly person in your life, but strive for a close relationship with at least one or two of these people. In the form of a prayer, write down your commitment to get everything you can from the godly people in your life.

## Prayer

*Dear Lord, thank you for your Word. I don't want to be guilty of wasting an opportunity. I realize that there are godly people in my life that I'm taking for granted. I am not learning all that I could be. Please give me the wisdom to grow as much as I can from those you have put in my life. In Jesus' name I pray, Amen.*

# WEEKEND WARRIOR
## Manasseh
### Read 2 Chronicles 33:10–24

t's terribly sad to hear the stories of former members of my youth group who have drifted from the Lord. Some have been through so much: unplanned pregnancies, drug addiction, crime, prison, near-death experiences. I thank God that most of these people (but not all) appear to be in a humbled state of mind. They have come to realize that they cannot fight God and win.

No matter what you do, God is God. He always was and will always be the Supreme Being. He will not be dethroned. Consequently, His Word will never pass away. If you sin but do not repent and ask God's forgiveness, you will pay for it, dearly. It's awful that people have to go through so much before they realize this.

*Do not be deceived, God is not mocked; for whatever a man sows, that he will also reap. For he who sows to his flesh will of the flesh reap corruption, but he who sows to the Spirit will of the Spirit reap everlasting life.*

*—Galatians 6:7–8*

Once Manasseh was deported and imprisoned, he repented. He realized that God was not messing around. He realized that he did not have more power than God and could not do whatever he wanted. Manasseh's circumstances humbled him and helped him realize how wrong he was.

*Now when [Manasseh] was in affliction, he implored the Lord his God, and humbled himself greatly before the God of his fathers, and prayed to Him; and He received his entreaty, heard his supplication, and brought him back to Jerusalem into his kingdom.*

*Then Manasseh knew that the Lord was God.*

*—2 Chronicles 33:12–13*

When Manasseh returned to Jerusalem, he tried to undo the evil he had done but soon found out it was too late. Manasseh's evil son Amon decided that he wanted to live like his dad. As a result, the fruit of Manasseh's wickedness continued to affect people long after he was dead. His legacy was corrupted forever.

*Amon was twenty-two years old when he became king, and he reigned two years in Jerusalem. But he did evil in the sight of the Lord, as his father Manasseh had done; for Amon sacrificed to all the carved images which his father Manasseh had made, and served them.*

*—verses 21–22*

You don't have to wait until you go through a near-death experience to repent and get your life in order. First John 1:9 says, "If we confess our sins, He is faithful and just to forgive us our sins and to cleanse us from all unrighteousness." Today you can make a decision to learn from the Manassehs of the world and repent. Look around at all the people who have done things their own way and you will see that no one can fight God and win. You cannot go against God's Word without suffering the consequences.

## Interaction

List five people you know who have tried to fight God and win. Write down their acts of rebelliousness and God's resulting consequences. Then add yourself to the list. What sin of choice are you holding on to as you fight God, and what consequences have you begun to experience?

## Prayer

*Dear Lord, thank you for your Word. I repent now of my rebellious spirit. I want to become your servant now. I want to follow you now. I humble myself now; I don't want to wait until I go through a near-death experience before I get right with you. In Jesus' name I pray, Amen.*

# WEEK 13

## Be a Leader Like Gideon

Imagine your entire country being oppressed by another country for seven years. No one can stop it. All of a sudden you are picked by God to lead the way to change. What would you do? Would you accept the challenge to be leader or run away?

This is the story of Gideon, a young man who accepted the challenge and blossomed into the leader his country desperately needed. But how could a young man lead his country out of bondage? What lessons about leadership can we learn from Gideon's story?

This week the Holy Spirit will challenge you to be a bad-to-the-bone leader like Gideon, a leader whom God can use to bring about change in the world. May God bless you as you study His Word.

# Memory Verse
# of the Week

Let no one despise your youth, but be an example to the believers in word, in conduct, in love, in spirit, in faith, in purity.

1 TIMOTHY 4:12

# MONDAY
## Follow the Leader
### Read Judges 6–7

During my high school years, every Wednesday during the summer my buddies and I would hang out in a nearby park and see bands perform on a portable stage. The free concerts attracted thousands of people.

One time about five of us were walking toward the concert area when a group of older kids confronted us. For some reason they singled out my friend Tyrone and tried to intimidate him. Not wanting a fight, we just did our best to ignore them and quickly walked away.

"Why'd they get in *my* face?" Tyrone asked us later.

We didn't know it at the time, but I think they picked him out from the group because he appeared to be our leader. Tyrone had been walking ahead of us, and the definition of a leader is someone who is being followed.

We must always remember that there are bad-to-the-bone leaders and there are bad leaders. Gideon was a bad-to-the-bone leader who people followed into good battles—battles that honored God.

The Midianites had abused and oppressed the Jews for many years. But when God called Gideon to lead an army to fight them, the army followed. Once Gideon accepted the calling to be a leader, his actions spoke, "Follow me, fellas, I'll show you how it's done."

If you are not being followed, you are not a leader. You are just going for a walk. If you are going to be a leader like Gideon, God's going to guide you into a spiritual battle of some sort. And He will use you as someone others will follow. Not only will others follow you to the place of the battle but they will follow your example on how to fight in the battle.

You may already be acting as a leader in your life. Look around and see if there are people following your lead. It could be on an athletic team, in your classroom, or on your job. If you are acting as a leader now, you have a responsibility to develop and use those leadership skills for the good of God's kingdom. Your godliness can be an example for others to follow.

If you have not identified your leadership abilities, now is a perfect time to begin praying about them. It is possible to learn and develop leadership skills. Spend some time in prayer about becoming a leader like Gideon.

## Interaction

In what ways do people follow your example? Are you setting godly or ungodly examples?

## Prayer

*Dear Lord, thank you for your Word. I pray that I would be a godly example for others to follow, and I pray that I would notice in what ways I am being followed that don't honor you. Change me so that I may truly be a bad-to-the-bone leader like Gideon. In Jesus' name I pray, Amen.*

## Memory Verse

Let no one despise your youth, but be an example to the believers in word, in conduct, in love, in spirit, in faith, in purity.

1 Timothy 4:12

# TUESDAY

## A Leader's Leader

### Read Judges 6:1–16

One day during a senior class trip to New York City, a group of kids walking down Fifth Avenue found a wrapped box with a diamond ring inside. The attached card had a name but no address or phone number. The kids—some Christians, some not—began to argue about what to do.

A pawn shop was nearby, so one kid suggested they see how much they could get for the ring. The pawn shop was ready to buy it for one thousand dollars, but just before closing the deal, one of the Christian kids spoke up: "We should wait and not sell it." They continued to argue until the class president, who was also a leader in her youth group, asked a very important question: "What would Jesus do?"

She concluded that Jesus would pray and ask His Father for direction, so that's what she did. After praying, she decided to look up the person's name in the phone book. She knew the incredible odds of finding the owner in a city of ten million people, but she did find the rightful owner. And when the ring was returned, she received a two-thousand-dollar reward!

Bad-to-the-bone leaders must be committed to following Jesus simply because our ways are not God's ways. When Gideon was called to lead the army into battle, he desperately needed direction and wisdom from the Father. Gideon wasn't going to repeat the mistakes and evildoings of Israel's past, which had led to the oppression in the first place.

*Then the children of Israel did evil in the sight of the Lord. So the Lord delivered them into the hand of Midian for seven years, and the hand of Midian prevailed against Israel. Because of the*

*Midianites, the children of Israel made for themselves the dens, the caves, and the strongholds which are in the mountains.*

*—Judges 6:1–2*

If you want to lead God's people, God must lead you. Gideon's attitude was *Go ahead, Lord. Wherever you go, I am right behind you. I must decrease, and You must increase* (John 3:30).

You must be open to doing everything God's way, in His timing, and with the people He gives you. There simply is no better way of being a leader.

## Interaction

When was the last time God told you to do something His way, but you ignored His request because in your eyes it didn't make sense? Make a commitment that the next time God leads you to lead or make an "oddball" decision, you will trust Him.

## Prayer

*Dear Lord, thank you for your Word. I pray that I will not fear being a leader, because I know that I'd only be following you. I know that I am walking in the dark if you are not ahead of me. As Psalm 119:105 says, "Your word is a lamp to my feet and a light to my path." I surrender my heart to you and pray that you would speak clearly so that I may know the direction you want me to lead your people. Please make me be a bad-to-the-bone leader like Gideon. In Jesus' name I pray, Amen.*

## Memory Verse

Let no one despise your youth, but be an example to the believers in word, in conduct, in love, in spirit, in faith, in purity.

1 Timothy 4:12

# WEDNESDAY

## Ready, Set, Go!

### Read Judges 7

D o you have a friend who always has to be first in no matter what? First to get the hot new shoes. First to be called upon in class. First to be accepted by a college.

All too often people equate being first with being a leader. Sometimes leaders lead by serving or encouraging others; thus, they're not always first in line. But godly leaders are always first when it comes to obedient action. As a leader, when God tells you to go, you need to go.

When God told Gideon that he was going to fight the Midianites, he immediately got up early the next morning and acted. He did not sit around complaining and whining, he acted. God asked Gideon to challenge those who were fearful to go home.

*"Now therefore, proclaim in the hearing of the people, saying, 'Whoever is fearful and afraid, let him turn and depart at once from Mount Gilead.'" And twenty-two thousand of the people returned, and ten thousand remained.*

*—Judges 7:3*

Undoubtedly Gideon was a little nervous, especially when God next told Gideon to challenge his men to drink water out of the river. Even though it seemed like an odd command, Gideon did it immediately. He also acted immediately when God finally told Gideon to sneak around the back and attack with an ambush. And it worked.

Basically, when God told Gideon to jump, he jumped—and did not come down until God said so. If you are going to be a leader like Gideon, you will have to learn to act immediately. The Bible says that more than anything God desires obedience. In fact, He equates disobedience with witchcraft (1 Samuel 15:22–23).

At the start of each day, decide that you will act as soon as God gives the command, no matter what.

## Interaction

Think of one thing that God has told you to do that you have put off (for example, being more consistent in reading your Bible or praying, volunteering at church, apologizing to someone). Write it down and then write the word "obedient" next to it.

## Prayer

*Dear Lord, thank you for your Word. I pray that I would practice immediate obedience to you in my life. I know that I hurt myself and you when you give me a command and I tell you to wait before I will obey. Please give me the courage and discipline to be an obedient, bad-to-the-bone leader like Gideon. In Jesus' name I pray, Amen.*

## Memory Verse

Let no one despise your youth, but be an example to the believers in word, in conduct, in love, in spirit, in faith, in purity.

1 Timothy 4:12

# THURSDAY

## No Fear

### Read Judges 6:25–32

As you know by now, I was raised in a pretty strict home. Talking back to my parents or any authority figure was unheard of. I also attended a very strict elementary school with strict nuns who enforced the law.

One day I let my friends push me into asking my dad for the car. I knew he'd never let me borrow it, but they convinced me that if I just kept on his case he'd eventually let me borrow it just to get me out of his hair. I nervously walked into the house and found my dad in the back room, reading his paper. "Dad, can I borrow the car?"

He grunted a quick no.

"Oh, come on, Dad, let me have the car."

He pulled the newspaper down very slowly and looked me in the eye. As he did my knees were shaking, my heart was pounding, and I was sweating all over, wondering how quickly he was going to jump out of the chair. Five seconds of silence felt like an hour. Then, to my shock, he said, "Okay, go ahead." I was happy to be alive, let alone get the car. My father wouldn't have really killed me, but it was definitely a scary situation.

Imagine how Gideon felt when he was told by God to tear down his father's altar, which Joash had built to worship his god Baal. Gideon feared and respected his dad, but he obeyed God and tore it down that night when no one was around. But even though he did it at night, he knew in the morning his dad would wake up and discover what he had done. Undoubtedly, he worried what his father would do, but his attitude was *My dad has to deal with God on this.*

Rather than fearing people, who can only kill our body, we should only fear God, who can kill our body and soul. When God calls you to do something, when God calls you to be a leader, you cannot afford to have any fear of man. This is a quality that Gideon had, a quality that God reinforced by asking him to tear down his father's altar.

When God calls you, He's going to challenge you to stand up to people you might be intimidated by. You're going to have to faithfully obey God in the face of that fear, and do what God has called you to do. My challenge to you is not to fear any earthly person. Fear only God, and don't let anyone cause you to back down from obeying Him.

## Interaction

Write down the name of one person who intimidates you from walking with God. It may be the person you're scared to share the Gospel with, someone you're embarrassed to carry your Bible in front of, or someone you may be intimidated to pray with.

## Prayer

*Dear Lord, thank you for your Word. Thank you for the example of Gideon, who was a young man who did not fear other humans. I pray that I will never fear man or be intimidated by man to the point of not obeying what you have called me to do. I pray that this week I could be a bad-to-the-bone leader like Gideon. In Jesus' name I pray, Amen.*

## Memory Verse

Let no one despise your youth, but be an example to the believers in word, in conduct, in love, in spirit, in faith, in purity.

1 Timothy 4:12

# FRIDAY

## Fearless Friend

### Read Judges 7:9–25

If you're like most teenagers, you've had at least one, if not two jobs in your teen years. And as an employee, you were probably forced to do things you didn't want to do. You had to sweep floors, clean toilets, rake leaves, etc. Every now and then, would you look at the boss and wonder what he or she did?

I know that when I was a kid I always dreamed about being the boss. I figured that as boss I would make all the money, get to boss everybody around, and just kick back. But I realized this wasn't true the day I visited a friend of mine who was the head of a large ministry.

More than one hundred people work in his ministry. He touches a lot of people. I wanted to start a ministry, too, so I asked him for advice. About halfway through our conversation he hung his head and began to open up to me and cry. He shared with me all the burdens that he was carrying. He shared all the criticism he had to take every day. All the responsibility he had and his great need for encouragement.

As a leader, you will need someone to encourage you. God will never call you to walk alone. First of all, God will never leave you or forsake you (Deuteronomy 31:6). He wants to be your strength, your wisdom, and your guidance. He wants to be the only foundation you stand on. But God also wants to send people into your life to support you.

When Gideon was called to fight the Midianites, he was originally given thirty-three thousand men, and after God weeded out all the wrong people, he was left with only three hundred soldiers to fight an entire army. But during the battle God made sure Gideon received encouragement.

*If you are afraid to go down, go down to the camp with Purah, your servant, and you shall hear what they say. And afterwards your hands shall be strengthened.*

*—Judges 7:10*

God will always provide someone to encourage you and lift you up. As a leader you should look for that person. Someone who believes in God's calling on your life to be a leader; someone who is called to support and encourage you and pray for you; someone who is called to back you up when everyone else turns their backs on you.

God always knows the challenges He's going to put before you, and He knows just how much pressure you can take. He also knows just the right person to be there to encourage you, and if that person isn't there, He knows how to encourage you himself. So never think that you have to do it alone. If you're going to be a good leader, you're going to need to receive from God His encouragement and His pat on the back.

## Interaction

Write down the name of a person who encourages you or believes in you as a leader.

## Prayer

*Dear Lord, thank you for your Word. Thank you that in your Word you provide all the wisdom and counsel we need to do the things you have called us to do. I pray as a young, growing leader that you would send people into my life to encourage my leadership skills. I need encouragement to bear the burden of being first in line; encourage me to be a person of action and a person of obedience. I know with that encouragement, whether it comes from a person or from you, that I will be a bad-to-the-bone leader like Gideon. In Jesus' name I pray, Amen.*

## Memory Verse

Let no one despise your youth, but be an example to the believers in word, in conduct, in love, in spirit, in faith, in purity.

1 Timothy 4:12

# WEEKEND WARRIOR
## Jeremiah
### Read Jeremiah 1:1–5

The book of Jeremiah is about one of those faithful, beyond-belief prophets. No one ever listened to Jeremiah—no one believed his preaching—because he was called to deliver bad news to disobedient people. He preached repentance to people who would not listen.

This must have been extra difficult for Jeremiah to accept because when he was called into the ministry, he didn't think he'd be able to do it. When Jeremiah was starting out, his apparent fear was evident to the Lord when he said in Jeremiah 1:6, "Ah, Lord God! Behold, I cannot speak, for I am a youth."

What Jeremiah didn't realize was that his ministry did not begin when he was a young man. As a matter of fact, it began before he was born. It started when God appointed Jeremiah even before he was formed in the womb.

*"Before I formed you in the womb I knew you; before you were born I sanctified you; I ordained you a prophet to the nations."*
*—Jeremiah 1:5*

Guess what? Your ministry began before you were born, because that's when God designed and created you. God knows everything about you. He formed you and made you. He gave you spiritual abilities.

*For we are His workmanship, created in Christ Jesus for good works, which God prepared beforehand that we should walk in them.*
*—Ephesians 2:10*

God not only made you, but He also made the opportunities you'll face. This is all part of being chosen. The most important thing to remember about fulfilling your calling is that you're inadequate to do it alone. There must be supernatural intervention in your life. Just as God intervened in *making* you, so He must intervene in *using* you. The only way for this to happen—for God to make up the difference between your abilities and inabilities—is to trust God by faith.

2 Corinthians 5:7 says that we are to "walk by faith, not by sight." You must know and believe that you have been perfectly made to walk the road that is ahead, only by faith. Your abilities will only be maximized if you walk by faith and surrender them to God by faith. Faith is God-dependence, and this only begins when self-dependence ends. As Hebrews 11:1 says, "Faith is the substance of things hoped for and evidence of things unseen." Remember, if you are chosen you must choose faith.

## Interaction

List three things you find yourself inadequate to do unless you do them by faith. Make a commitment to continue to trust God.

## Prayer

*Dear Lord, thank you for your Word. I realize that you have formed me just the way I should be for the job you have appointed for me. But I also realize that in order for me to complete the task ahead, I must live by faith. I pray I will not underestimate the significance of your calling on my life or the power of living by faith. My prayer today is that I will never think I'm too young to be used by you and that I'll always remember that I have been chosen like Jeremiah. In Jesus' name I pray, Amen.*

# WEEKEND WARRIOR
## Jeremiah
### Read Jeremiah 1:6–10

One of the most common fears people have when taking on a challenge is that they will fail. It's especially easy to be fearful when you're trying to do something for the Lord and everyone around you believes something different.

It's an awesome responsibility to represent God in life. In Jeremiah's entire ministry he never had one convert. As a matter of fact, he lived a very sad life with a broken heart and was rejected by the very people he set out to help.

No matter what happens, you cannot give up simply because your job is to be who God made you to be. You are to do what God has called you to do. You can never be anything different.

In difficult times, here are two things that will help you persevere:

🏃 First, stay faithful to preaching and living God's Word.

When Jeremiah expressed fear about not being listened to, Jeremiah 1:9 says, "The Lord put forth His hand and touched my mouth, and the Lord said to me: 'Behold, I have put My words in your mouth.'"

When you begin to do something for the Lord, there are a thousand reasons why people won't listen to you. It may be that you're not preaching a popular, easy-to-swallow message. Perhaps you're not entertaining enough, or don't sound very convincing. It doesn't matter much whether these things are true or not. Unless God touches your mouth with His purifying coal, nothing you say will amount to anything. Let God touch your mouth. Ask Him to give you His words, His anointing, His insight, and His power. Ask Him to give you wisdom in what to say, how to say it, and when to say it. Doing this is an act of submission to His leading, guiding, and forming the words that come out of your mouth.

✗ Second, find a partner in ministry.

Whatever God has called you to do, always know that someone in your school, church, or neighborhood is dealing with the same problems and pressures in his/her life. Someone has heard of you and wants to be used in a mighty way also. There is someone who can relate to your pressures, worries, and concerns about those you're trying to minister to.

Jeremiah knew King Josiah, the teenage king who brought about spiritual reform to his nation. History tells us that they were friends. Pray that God would bring someone into your life—a soul mate, a prayer partner—who you can share any pains and frustrations with.

## Interaction

Write out the top three frustrations you have in your relationship with Christ. Then write how God has dealt with them in the past (knowing that His dealing with you this way is a sign of His calling on your life).

## Prayer

*Dear Lord, thank you for your Word. My prayer today is that you would touch my mouth with your hand. I ask that I would trust in the power of your Word. I pray that no matter what people say or do, I will be faithful. Help me realize that it's my job to speak and do what you command, and leave the rest to you. I pray that I can live like I am chosen like Jeremiah. In Jesus' name I pray, Amen.*